JOY *the* BAKER

OVER EASY

JOY *the* BAKER

OVER EASY

Sweet and Savory Recipes *for* Leisurely Days

JOY WILSON

PHOTOGRAPHS BY JON MELENDEZ

Clarkson Potter/Publishers
New York

Published in the United States by Clarkson Potter/
Publishers, an imprint of the Crown Publishing Group, a
division of Penguin Random House LLC, New York.
crownpublishing.com
clarksonpotter.com

CLARKSON POTTER is a trademark and POTTER with
colophon is a registered trademark of Penguin Random
House LLC.

Library of Congress Cataloging-in-Publication Data
Names: Wilson, Joy, 1981– author.
Title: Joy the baker over easy: sweet and savory recipes for
leisurely days / Joy Wilson.
Description: First edition. | New York : Clarkson Potter,
an imprint of the Crown Publishing Group, a division of
Penguin Random House LLC, [2017] | Includes index.
Identifiers: LCCN 2016014019| ISBN 9780385345750
(hardcover : alk. paper) ISBN 9780385345767 (ebook)
Subjects: LCSH: Cooking. | LCGFT: Cookbooks.
Classification: LCC TX714 .W5255 2017 | DDC 641.5—dc23
LC record available at https://lccn.loc.gov/2016014019

ISBN 978-0-385-34575-0
eBook ISBN 978-0-385-34576-7

Printed in China

Book design by La Tricia Watford
Cover design by Jan Derevjanik
Interior and cover photographs by Jon Melendez

10 9 8 7 6 5 4 3 2 1

First Edition

FOR AMOS

I'll make the eggs, if you make the coffee.

CONTENTS

INTRODUCTION

What's your morning ritual? Depends on the demands of the day, doesn't it? Depends on if your alarm clock blared unexpectedly, sending you crashing into a Wednesday morning full of tisks and tasks, or if you eased into a Saturday, brought to life by the smell of your love making you coffee. Vastly different days, different feels, and different rituals.

On a typical day, I find myself scurrying to answer emails and manage my website as the water for my coffee boils. While making grocery lists and planning recipes for the week, I rather mindlessly sip caffeine into my body, likely neglecting even to make myself a piece of toast. It's not the most terrible of rituals; it's just more hurried and far less intentional than I'd like, because Wednesdays simply have a hearty momentum that's hard to keep up with.

Weekend mornings (or very extraordinary self-appointed vacation Thursdays) are something special. When the alarm isn't set to begin with and the ding of correspondence is silenced for many morning hours. It's in this space that a perfect meal—and the perfect reason to connect—exists. It's somewhere between breakfast and lunch, where eggs and toast meet gooey pastries, hot coffee, and boozy juice. It's called brunch, the most decadent and leisurely of meals. It creates its own energy that moves at the speed of flipping pancakes and poaching eggs and is when all is exactly as it should be.

My favorite brunch scene—the moment I daydream about on hectic mornings—is as the follows: A cup of black coffee made by my love. He sits at the counter while I make Bacon Pancakes (page 91) and perfect scrambled eggs (page 55). He mixes up Peach and Orange Palomas (page 15), and we sit at the counter and eat and chatter for what is likely an hour. It's a lazy and collaborative effort that stretches into the early afternoon with not a care in the world aside from now and pancakes.

There is a certain hedonism associated with brunch. It's a beautiful blending of morning and midday where everything is fair game. And it's celebratory, whether you're reminiscing over last night's third (or fourth) cocktail followed by french fries and pizza (that were entirely celebratory in their own right) or simply enjoying the fact of a day without a long list of to-dos. Sleeping in well into sunshiney mornings is just the nature of early Sundays. Whisking together eggs and cream, baking bacon with sugar, stirring juice with booze—on such leisurely weekend days, these things are not only acceptable and appropriate, they're part of a coveted and precious time when loves and friends are called over and afternoons are revered for their sluggishness.

That being said, I firmly believe that no one should stand in line for brunch. Afternoon eggs, without waiting among the hip and trendy, should be a luxury available to each and every one of us. Since the concept of brunching shows no signs of slowing (and, really, why should it?!), this book is our tool, our free pass to the front of the brunch line—just better, because we're at home, maybe in our pajamas, and who knows (or cares) what's going on with our bedhead.

Joy the Baker Over Easy is meant to celebrate and facilitate our own lazy meal days. The recipes here will satisfy any craving, whether you like things simple or decadent, savory or sweet. I've given lots of tips for how to make the very best eggs (however you like them), moist muffins, perfect coffee, and anything else that could make your brunch dream complete. Conveniently enough, and because no one should be left out of such a club, the dishes here are for "morning people," "afternoon people," and "breakfast for dinner people," with plenty of sandwiches, salads, and cocktails included. Brunch does not discriminate. Brunch isn't looking at the clock. Brunch just wants you to sit, relax, and enjoy a runny egg.

Welcome to it. Gather your eggs and let's get going!

COCKTAILS

AND COFFEE

There is a marked difference between Tuesday morning coffee and Saturday morning coffee. Tuesday morning coffee, if you're anything like me, is sipped gingerly from a travel mug in the car, rushing and likely ten minutes late for something. I probably couldn't even tell you what that coffee tasted like; I just know it's hot, brown, and buzzing with energy. Tuesday morning coffee is more necessity than enjoyment, which, though a shame, makes Saturday morning coffee that much more enjoyable.

Saturday morning coffee is the cup I get to savor. The level of care taken with that coffee is what separates a simple breakfast (that's likely eaten in a hurry) from a decadent brunch. I'm not talking about fine teacups or linen napkins with napkin rings but simply about attention to detail and the time spent that makes a morning meal special.

This chapter is all about time, care, and celebration in drink form. I like to make everything from refreshing herbaceous lemonades to sherbet punches and boozy treats—and so I've shared them all. An indulgent cup of coffee just for you, or a big tipsy punch for many. Every recipe has an interesting twist, and it's these layers of effort that make the morning meal noteworthy—and worth spending our day enjoying. Brunch calls for cocktails. Tuesday not so much, unless it's an emergency or tax season.

MICHELADAS FOR MANY

SERVES 6

It would be a mistake to think of the michelada as a beer-substituted Bloody Mary. That doesn't do justice to this delicious chameleon of a drink. Micheladas are popular in their home country, Mexico, where they're made every which way from Sunday. Some versions are a simple mixture of beer, lime, and salt, while others are a more complex blend of clam juice, spice, and chicken stock. For me, the essential components are a good Mexican lager (like Negra Modelo), chilled tomato juice, and, yes, clam juice, if even just a splash. That hint of sea flavor makes a michelada special. My recipe also calls for a few extra dashes of hot sauce, as well as Old Bay seasoning to complement the clam juice. Savory, slightly effervescent, and spicy. Serve with the Breakfast Burrito (page 182) or the Breakfast Burger (page 156). (See photograph, page 10.)

1. In a large pitcher, combine the tomato juice, clam juice, lime juice, Worcestershire sauce, hot sauce, soy sauce, and Old Bay. Stir well. Taste and add more lime juice or hot sauce as desired. Stir in the beer.

2. Fill six glasses with ice and divide the michelada among the glasses. Garnish with the pickled carrots, pickled jalapeños, and lime wedges.

3 cups chilled tomato juice

½ cup clam juice (I like Bar Harbor)

Juice of 3 limes, plus more to taste

2 teaspoons Worcestershire sauce

2 teaspoons hot sauce, plus more to taste

2 teaspoons soy sauce

1½ teaspoons Old Bay seasoning

3 (12-ounce) bottles chilled Mexican lager

Ice

Pickled carrots, for garnish

Pickled jalapeños, for garnish

Lime wedges, for garnish

PEACH AND ORANGE PALOMA

SERVES 4

A paloma is a classic tequila cocktail often overshadowed by the better-known margarita, but margaritas aren't the only way to combine tequila and citrus. My paloma is a classy combination of sweet orange and tequila, with the addition of fresh peach and a little fizz to dress it in its summer finest just for brunch. This is the sweetest way to sneak tequila onto the breakfast table. You're welcome.

½ teaspoon grated orange zest

¼ cup kosher salt

2 tablespoons sugar

3 tablespoons fresh lime juice, plus more to rim the glasses

2 cups fresh orange juice

1 ripe peach, pitted and coarsely chopped

Ice

8 ounces silver tequila

Club soda, chilled

Orange, peach, and lime slices, for garnish

1. In a small bowl, combine the orange zest, salt, and sugar. Using your fingers, work the zest into the salt and sugar until the mixture is fragrant. Place on a shallow plate.

2. Coat the rim of four glasses with lime juice. Gently dip the rim of each glass into the salt mixture and set aside.

3. In a blender, combine the lime juice, the orange juice, and the peach chunks. Blend until relatively smooth, about 1 minute. Pour into a fine-mesh strainer placed over a medium bowl. Press the peach pulp through the strainer, leaving behind any large pulp and peach skin pieces.

4. Fill each of the prepared glasses with ice. Pour 2 ounces of tequila into each glass. Top with ½ cup of the juice mixture. Top with club soda, and stir. Garnish with fruit slices, and serve.

APEROL SPRITZ

SERVES 6

An Italian liqueur flavored with both bitter and sweet orange, a plethora of herbs, and a hint of rhubarb, Aperol is a refreshing apéritif that's a pleasing start to a meal. It is similar to Campari but with less alcohol and less bitterness, making it friendlier to bitter-orange novices. Paired with sparkling prosecco and orange slices, this is festively colored, lightly boozy brunch perfection.

Fill six tall Collins glasses (or any sort of glass will be fine) with ice. Fill each glass halfway with prosecco. Add 1 ounce of Aperol to each glass. Top with club soda, garnish with an orange slice, stir lightly, and enjoy!

Ice

1 bottle (750ml) dry prosecco, chilled

6 ounces Aperol

Club soda, chilled

6 orange slices, for garnish

WATERMELON-MINT SANGRIA

Get thee a melon baller. Do it because it's the tool of a loving grandmother and a hard-core bruncher. Do it because a summer sangria, with fresh watermelon juice *and* actual watermelon balls, shows your dedication to delicious, refreshing, and beautiful brunch beveraging. I've had the best results using a juicer to make fresh watermelon juice. If you don't have a juicer, I've also had success making watermelon juice in a blender by first blending the fruit, and then straining it through a fine-mesh strainer. I love drinking this with my Pea and Goat Cheese Tortilla (page 78) or Chicken Avocado Arepas (page 180).

4 cups fresh watermelon juice

Handful of fresh mint leaves and stems

1 bottle (750ml) dry rosé wine

1 cup vodka

1 cup fresh orange juice

½ cup orange liqueur (such as Cointreau)

1 orange, sliced into rounds

1 lime, sliced into rounds

16 to 20 watermelon balls

Ice (optional)

1. Put the watermelon juice in a large pitcher or punch bowl. Add the mint and muddle slightly to release the flavor. Stir in the wine, vodka, orange juice, and orange liqueur.

2. Add the orange slices, lime slices, and watermelon balls. Refrigerate for at least 2 hours before serving. Serve over ice, if you'd like it extra cold.

SUMMER PIMM'S CUP
COCKTAIL

SERVES 6

Living in New Orleans in mid-August is like taking up residence in a 200-year-old wet sauna filled with music, laughter, life, and a steady rotation of well-iced and heavily garnished cocktails. It's heaven (if heaven had a steamy, torturous component). Even though the Pimm's Cup has British roots, it is the summertime cocktail jewel of this city, made famous at the Napoléon House in the French Quarter. My version is spiked with more gin than theirs, and it's heavily garnished with fresh fruit and cucumber, making it part cocktail, part salad. If you make it through the rest of summer to August in New Orleans, you've earned as many as you'd like.

I English cucumber, sliced

I cup hulled and sliced strawberries

I lemon, sliced into rounds

Handful of fresh mint stems and leaves

I cup gin

1½ cups Pimm's No. I

3 cups sparkling lemonade, chilled

Ice

1. In a large pitcher combine half of the cucumber slices, and all of the strawberries, lemon slices, and mint. Add the gin and Pimm's and stir well. Refrigerate for 2 hours, until chilled through.

2. Just before serving, stir in the sparkling lemonade. Fill six tall glasses with ice and pour the cocktail, as well as a bit of fruit, into each glass. Garnish with the remaining cucumber slices, and serve.

GRAPEFRUIT ROSEMARY MIMOSA

SERVES 8

This play on the traditional orange juice mimosa results in a slightly bitter, herbal concoction—as if champagne needs any fuss at all. It doesn't, but when it comes to brunch, more is more. And the pretty pink color next to the deep-green sprigs of rosemary is a stunner.

ROSEMARY SYRUP

1 cup water

1 cup sugar

3 fresh rosemary sprigs, plus smaller sprigs for garnish

1 bottle (750ml) dry champagne, chilled

2 cups fresh grapefruit juice, plus more as needed

1. **FOR THE ROSEMARY SYRUP:** In a small saucepan set over medium heat, bring the water and sugar to a simmer. Add the rosemary sprigs and stir. Remove the pan from the heat, cover, and let steep for 15 minutes. Remove the rosemary sprigs and discard.

2. To serve, fill eight glasses just under half full with champagne. Top each with about ¼ cup of grapefruit juice and 2 teaspoons of rosemary syrup. Add a bit more juice or champagne, whichever you prefer. Garnish with the smaller rosemary sprigs, and serve.

STRAWBERRY, GRAPEFRUIT, AND CHAMOMILE
BRUNCH PUNCH

SERVES 10 TO 12

Punch can be a rather simple, low-brow, and delicious affair that celebrates juice and mounds of sweet sherbet (Orange Sherbet Mimosa Punch, page 27), or it can be a more high-brow beverage of floral tea and bourbon. This summery, bright punch is feminine and sweet, but it's no wilting flower, thanks to a proper dose of bourbon. And really, if you're going to make a beauty of a punch, an ice mold decorated with frozen fruit and flowers is very fitting.

1. **FOR THE CHAMOMILE SYRUP:** Combine the water and sugar in a small saucepan set over medium heat. Bring to a simmer, stirring until the sugar is dissolved. Remove the pan from the heat, add the tea bags, and stir. Cover and let steep for 15 minutes. Remove the tea bags and discard. Refrigerate until room temperature or chilled, at least 1 hour.

2. **FOR THE PUNCH:** In a blender, combine the grapefruit juice and half of the strawberries. Blend until smooth. Pour the mixture into a large punch bowl. Add the chamomile syrup, bourbon, and bitters. Add the remaining strawberry slices and ice.

3. To serve, put a few ice cubes into serving cups, garnish with fresh flowers, if available, and ladle the punch into glasses.

CHAMOMILE SYRUP

3 cups water

2½ cups sugar

8 chamomile tea bags

PUNCH

4 cups fresh grapefruit juice

I pint fresh strawberries, hulled and sliced

3 cups bourbon

A few good dashes of bitters

Ice cubes or an ice mold, for serving

Fresh chamomile flowers, for garnish (optional)

MIMOSA PUNCH

SERVES 8 TO 10

I'll be the first to admit that the hardest part of making punch is figuring out in the way-back of which closet the punch bowl is hiding. It's not often that I dig out the punch bowl, but every time I do, it's worth it. To best serve this beverage, make sure all the ingredients are pre-chilled, since very cold liquids will help the frozen sherbet live longer. Assemble just before your guests arrive, and scoop and serve in enthusiastic portions.

In a large punch bowl, gently stir together the champagne, orange juice, and ginger ale. Add the orange sherbet in generous scoops. The sherbet will slowly melt into the punch. Ladle into rocks glasses (they're easier to ladle into than champagne flutes).

1 bottle (750ml) chilled dry champagne

4 cups chilled fresh orange juice

2 cups chilled ginger ale

1½ quarts orange sherbet

KALIMOTXO

SERVES 4

A Kalimotxo (pronounced cal-ee-MO-cho) elicits one of two reactions: a raised eyebrow in suspicion at both the pronunciation and ingredient list, or a knowing nod of the head in remembrance of post-college backpacking trips through Spain. One part red wine. One part cane-sugar cola. A lot of crushed ice. A good squeeze of lime. Opt for a cheap red wine, like a Spanish Rioja or Italian table wine from Trader Joe's. Set your suspicions aside for this delicious afternoon brunch accompaniment.

Fill four glasses with lots of ice. Divide the red wine among the glasses, and top with the cola. Squeeze a lime wedge into each glass and garnish with a lime round.

Ice

2 cups red table wine

2 cups cane sugar cola (I prefer Boylan cola)

Lime wedges and rounds, for garnish

MARTINI SHOTS

You know those brunches that bring together two newly dating people and their closest couple friends? The kind of brunch where no one knows everyone, and everyone is a little stiff, very in need of coffee, and definitely hungry? You'll likely talk about how you met your significant other, what happened on the most recent episode of *Game of Thrones* (while someone covers their ears and hums loudly to prevent spoilers), and everyone's favorite Helen Hunt movie (*Twister,* of course). This slightly awkward and very charming brunch calls for the Brunch Martini Shot to level the playing field. Call it a collective exhale.

Ice

5 ounces vodka or gin

1 ounce dry vermouth

1½ to 2 ounces olive brine

6 large green olives, for garnish

1. Fill a cocktail shaker halfway with ice. Add the vodka, vermouth, and olive brine. Place the lid on the cocktail shaker and shake vigorously until the outside of the shaker is frosted and very cold.

2. Strain the mixture among six shot glasses, top each with an olive, and serve.

DILL PICKLE BLOODY MARY

SERVES 6

I imagine that if Alice had brunch in Wonderland, the Queen of Hearts would serve this cocktail in her finest teacups, on her finest linens. There'd be trippy petits fours and loopy quiches, and someone would surely lose their head. This twist on the classic Bloody Mary is made with a gut-shot of dill pickle juice and a special dill pickle–flavored vodka.

1. **FOR THE BLOODY MARY MIXTURE:** In a large pitcher, stir together the tomato juice, pickle juice, horseradish (use more if you prefer it spicy), lemon and lime juices, Worcestershire sauce, celery salt, salt, and pepper. Cover with plastic wrap and refrigerate for at least 1 hour.

2. To serve, fill six glasses with ice. Add 2 ounces of the Dill Pickle Vodka to each glass. Top with the Bloody Mary mixture and garnish as generously as you'd like. Enjoy immediately.

BLOODY MARY MIXTURE
36 ounces tomato juice

⅓ cup dill pickle juice

2 to 4 tablespoons prepared horseradish

2 tablespoons fresh lemon juice

2 tablespoons fresh lime juice

2 teaspoons Worcestershire sauce

¾ teaspoon celery salt

½ teaspoon salt

¼ teaspoon freshly cracked black pepper

Ice

Dill Pickle Vodka (recipe follows)

GARNISHES (optional)
Celery sticks

Pickled green beans

Pickled okra

Green olives

Crisp bacon slices

Lemon and lime wedges

DILL PICKLE VODKA

MAKES 4 CUPS

3 cups vodka
½ cup dill pickle juice
3 dill pickle spears

In a clear jar with a lid, combine the vodka, pickle juice, and pickle spears. Cover and refrigerate for 3 days before serving. The flavored vodka will keep for several weeks in the refrigerator.

HIBISCUS LIMEADE

SERVES 8

Made with dried hibiscus flowers (the kind that might get tucked behind your ear in Hawaii), this caffeine-free tea is mild, floral, and sweet, with just a touch of tartness. I always have a box of hibiscus tea bags on hand from the tea company Traditional Medicinals. Adjust the sweetness of this limeade to suit your taste, and try it with raw honey, if you prefer a natural sweetener.

5 hibiscus tea bags

10 cups water

1 cup sugar

⅔ cup fresh lime juice

Ice

Lime slices, for garnish

Fresh blackberries, for garnish

1. Place the tea bags in a large pitcher. Bring 3 cups of water to a boil and pour it into the pitcher. Stir in the sugar until it dissolves. Cover and let steep for 15 minutes. Remove the tea bags and discard.

2. Stir in the lime juice and the remaining 7 cups water. Refrigerate for at least 2 hours.

3. To serve, fill eight glasses with ice. Stir the limeade well before pouring into the glasses. Garnish with lime slices and blackberries.

HONEY-GINGER
SWEET TEA

SERVES 6

There's a big difference between sipping tea and spilling tea. The former is a lovely late-morning activity, properly undertaken on a Southern porch, sitting under a lazy fan, with ice melting in perspiring glasses. The latter is talking gossip, which also very often involves sitting under lazy fans on Southern porches. Come to think of it, sipping and spilling tea go hand in hand: refreshing, relaxing, with a splash of scandal.

6 cups boiling filtered water

4 black tea bags

½ to ¾ cup honey, depending on desired sweetness

2 tablespoons finely grated fresh ginger

Ice

Lemon slices, for garnish

1. In a large pitcher, combine the boiling water, tea bags, honey to taste, and ginger. Stir well and let steep for 5 minutes. Remove the tea bags, and if you'd like a smooth tea without the grated ginger, strain through a fine-mesh strainer. Refrigerate until cold, about 2 hours.

2. To serve, fill six tall glasses with ice. Pour the chilled tea into the glasses and garnish with lemon slices.

PINEAPPLE-CUCUMBER-MINT
AGUA FRESCA

SERVES 6 TO 8

You can find large jars of brightly colored agua fresca at taquerias all over Los Angeles. I like to think of this beverage as the more impassioned cousin of lemonade, because it's fruit-forward and totally adaptable. My version is bright with pineapple and mint—and it's completely refreshing. This recipe is flexible. For example, you can substitute strawberries for cucumber or ripe cantaloupe for the pineapple.

3 cups fresh pineapple chunks

½ English cucumber, sliced into chunks

I small handful fresh mint leaves, plus a few sprigs for garnish

½ cup sugar

5 cups filtered water

Ice

1. In a blender, combine the pineapple, cucumber, mint leaves, sugar, and 2 cups of water. Blend on high until smooth. The mixture will have a thick smoothie-like consistency. Pour the mixture into a pitcher and stir in the remaining 3 cups of water. Refrigerate for at least 2 hours.

2. To serve, fill six to eight glasses with ice. Divide the agua fresca among the glasses and garnish with mint sprigs.

FANCY ICE

Brunch is one of those extra-special weekend indulgences that's all about the details, right down to the ice cubes. Your game will definitely go up a few notches when you serve drinks with flavorful ice cubes that complement and enhance the beverage they keep cool. Imagine, melting ice cubes that enhance a drink, not dilute it! Here are some of my favorites. Most of these take about 6 hours to freeze completely solid.

LEMONADE ICE CUBES: Pour a batch of lemonade into an ice cube tray and add a small wedge of lemon to each cube and freeze. Try these in the Honey-Ginger Sweet Tea (page 36).

COFFEE ICE CUBES: Pour cooled black coffee into an ice cube tray and freeze. Try these in the Black and White Russian (page 51).

BLOODY MARY CUBES: In a measuring cup, combine tomato juice, a bit of black pepper, and a pinch or two of horseradish. Stir, pour into an ice cube tray, and freeze. Try in the Dill Pickle Bloody Mary (page 32).

CUCUMBER-JALAPEÑO CUBES: Juice 1 unpeeled cucumber and combine with 1 cup distilled water. Pour into an ice cube tray. Add thin slices of cucumber and thin slices of jalapeño to each cube and freeze. Try in the Pineapple-Cucumber-Mint Agua Fresca (page 38).

FRUIT SALAD CUBES: Put fresh raspberries, blueberries, sliced strawberries, and sliced kiwi in an ice cube tray. Pour distilled water over the fruit and freeze until frozen solid. These are great in the Summer Pimm's Cup Cocktail (page 20).

SHIRLEY TEMPLE CUBES: In a measuring cup, combine 1½ cups distilled water and ½ cup grenadine. Pour into an ice cube tray, filling each ¾ full. Add a maraschino cherry (with stem) to each cube and freeze. Try in the Kalimotxo (page 28).

BRUNCH PUNCH ICE MOLDS: Bring distilled water to a boil, and then let cool for 10 minutes. Fill ice cube trays with the water and freeze at least 6 hours or overnight, until solid. To make the ice mold, arrange sliced fruit (strawberries, grapefruit, peaches, or cucumber) at the bottom of the mold. Top with ice cubes made from distilled water (to keep the fruit from floating during freezing). Fill the mold three-quarters full with cold distilled water and freeze at least 6 hours or overnight, until solid. To loosen and release the ice, run the mold under warm water.

CUCUMBER, CELERY, ROMAINE, AND APPLE
JUICE

SERVES 2

Let's get our greens in and out of the way. Well, it's not like they're in the way; it's just that there are cheesy eggs to eat. This juice isn't heavy on the leafy greens and relies more on the hydrating efforts of cucumber and celery. A green juice on the lighter side, with a dose of sweetness from fresh apples. Now . . . please pass the cheesy eggs.

Because this recipe calls for vegetables and leafy greens, you'll need to use a pressing juicer. I'm afraid the blender has a hard time contending with celery.

Press the cucumber, celery, romaine, and apples through a juicer. Divide between two large ice-filled cups. Enjoy immediately, or keep refrigerated for up to 2 days.

1 English cucumber, sliced

5 celery stalks, trimmed

3 cups coarsely chopped romaine lettuce

2 Fuji apples, unpeeled, cored, and sliced

Ice

CARROT, BEET, CITRUS, AND SWEET POTATO
JUICE

SERVES 4

This juice is as powerful as it is magenta-hued. Full of beta-carotene, liver-detoxifying powers, tummy-soothing qualities, and vitamin C, it's a glorious way to fill our bodies with nutrients and beauty. This recipe requires a juicer, a kitchen luxury that really delivers. It's the only thing that will extract juice from hard root veggies such as sweet potatoes.

Press the carrots, beet, sweet potato, ginger, oranges, and grapefruit through a juicer. Divide among four ice-filled glasses and enjoy!

5 carrots, unpeeled, cut into bite-size pieces

I beet, unpeeled, trimmed, and cut into bite-size pieces

I large sweet potato, unpeeled, cut into bite-size pieces

2- to 3-inch piece of fresh ginger, unpeeled, chopped

2 navel oranges, peeled and cut into bite-size pieces

I grapefruit, peeled and cut into bite-size pieces

Ice

STRABERRY, PINEAPPLE, AND RASPBERRY
SMOOTHIE BOWL

MAKES 2 BOWLS

Some weekend mornings I wake up and want something pink that I can eat with a spoon. Instead of reaching into the freezer for the strawberry ice cream, I find this fruity smoothie bowl is the ticket. Brightly flavored with pineapple and tangy yogurt, it becomes sweet and pink thanks to strawberries and raspberries. This is probably as close as we should get to eating strawberry ice cream for brunch.

1. **FOR THE SMOOTHIE:** In a blender, combine the pineapple, strawberries, raspberries, almond milk, yogurt, protein powder, and water. Blend until thick but smooth (if it's too thick, add a little water).

2. Divide the smoothie between two small bowls and top generously with granola, goji berries, shredded coconut, and chia seeds, as desired.

SMOOTHIE

1 cup frozen pineapple chunks

Heaping ½ cup frozen strawberries

Heaping ½ cup frozen raspberries

½ cup almond milk

½ cup Greek yogurt

2 tablespoons protein powder

½ cup water, plus more as needed

TOPPINGS (optional)

Granola

Goji berries

Shredded coconut

Chia seeds

SPINACH, KALE, AND MANGO
SMOOTHIE BOWL

MAKES 2 BOWLS

Thick, spoonable smoothies topped with fresh fruit, granola, nuts, and seeds—these bowls are both beautiful and healthy. They have loads of greens, are sweetened with fruit, and are amped up with protein powder to make them that much more satisfying. I always go for a natural protein powder, like pea protein powder from Aloha. Bonus: these bowls make me feel like I've cheated and stopped for frozen yogurt before my morning coffee.

1. **FOR THE SMOOTHIE:** In a blender, combine the spinach, kale, mango, protein powder, and almond milk. Blend until thick but smooth (if it's too thick, add a little water).

2. Divide the smoothie between two small bowls and top generously with blueberries, kiwi, granola, and chia seeds, as desired.

SMOOTHIE

2 cups spinach leaves

I cup kale leaves, stems removed

I heaping cup frozen mango chunks

2 tablespoons protein powder

I cup almond milk

TOPPINGS (optional)

Blueberries

Sliced kiwi

Granola

Chia seeds

CASHEW, CINNAMON, BANANA, AND COCOA NIB
SMOOTHIE

SERVES 2

Consider this a creamy, chocolate-studded, health-crazed, pre-noon milkshake. Softened raw cashews, together with cinnamon and banana, create a satisfying, healthful morning beverage. The cocoa nibs add a bite of bitter chocolate. For extra pep, replace the water with chilled coffee (now we're talking!).

1 cup water

½ cup raw cashews

2 tablespoons honey

2 bananas, cut into chunks and frozen

¾ teaspoon ground cinnamon

3 tablespoons cocoa nibs

1½ cups cold filtered water

1. In a small bowl, combine the 1 cup of water and cashews. Let soak for 2 hours; drain.

2. In a blender, combine the soaked cashews, honey, bananas, cinnamon, cocoa nibs, and 1½ cups of cold filtered water. Blend until completely smooth. Divide between two glasses and serve immediately.

MANGO BUTTERMILK SMOOTHIE

SERVES 2

I used to think drinking buttermilk was for grandfathers who sat on back porches smoking pipes and listening to baseball games on the radio. Of course, this describes my buttermilk-drinking grandfather perfectly. Turns out, he was on to something. Sour milk (sour, not spoiled) is a deliciously tangy complement to sweet, ripe mango. If you don't have buttermilk on hand, substitute 1 cup plain yogurt and about ½ cup water.

In a blender, combine the buttermilk, banana, mango, honey, and nutmeg, and blend until smooth. Divide between two glasses and serve immediately.

1½ cups buttermilk

1 banana, cut into chunks and frozen

1½ cups ripe mango chunks

2 tablespoons honey

Pinch of freshly grated nutmeg

FROTHY, MILKY, AT-HOME MOCHAS

SERVES 2

Home lattes were really just glorified mugs of milky coffee until I tucked a few tricks under my belt. Since most of us don't have coffee shop–quality espresso machines at home, we have to know how to fake it. The essentials: coffee concentrate (an unsweetened, strong, concentrated coffee that mimics espresso), a mason jar with a lid, and 2% milk (you won't get good froth with 1% or skim).

3 cups 2% milk

¼ cup sugar

3 tablespoons unsweetened cocoa powder

1 tablespoon coconut oil

¼ to ⅓ cup coffee concentrate, depending on how strong you want it (I like Cool Brew and Chameleon Cold Brew)

1. To froth the milk, fill a mason jar halfway full with the milk. Place a lid on the jar and shake vigorously for about 1 minute, until the milk is bubbly, frothy, and has increased in volume. Remove the lid from the jar and microwave the milk until warm, 30 to 45 seconds. Repeat, if necessary, to froth and warm all of the milk.

2. To make the latte, divide the sugar and cocoa powder equally between two mugs. Stir to break up any lumps. Divide the coconut oil between the two mugs and stir until it is a thick paste. Add 2 to 3 tablespoons of coffee concentrate to each mug and stir well. Add ¼ cup of the warm milk to each mug, and stir until the sugar begins to dissolve. Add 1 cup more milk to each mug, stir, and then spoon foam over the tops. Serve warm.

MY FAVORITE WAY TO COFFEE

The first cup of coffee in the morning is important. Of course it's about flavor, temperature, and that much needed jolt of energy, but above all, morning coffee is a ritual. More often than not, the weekday routine involves a rushed cup, sipped sporadically while working away, ticking tasks off my to-do lists. For me, the coffee making and drinking are tasks in and of themselves. But brunch is no time for a rushed cup, sipped carefully while sitting in traffic. Brunch is when we slow down the morning get-up-and-go.

Here's my favorite way to make weekend coffee. For best results, I stay in my pajamas, put on my favorite songs from at least ten years ago (likely something by the Cranberries), and take my time. While this method is fussy, it's well worth the effort to make a very good cup or two of joe.

HERE'S WHAT I USE: Chemex 3-cup glass coffeemaker, paper filters, small kitchen scale with timer, burr grinder, electric kettle, and coffee—a very good, freshly roasted, whole coffee bean.

HERE'S HOW I MAKE IT: Bring water to a boil in the electric kettle. Meanwhile, weigh 25 grams of whole coffee beans for a single cup of coffee. Grind the beans. Fold the paper filter like coffee origami, creating a funnel for the coffee to slowly filter through (your coffeemaker should have instructions). Pour a little of the boiling water over the empty coffee filter in the coffeemaker to moisten and heat the coffeemaker. Discard the water. Set the coffeemaker on top of the scale.

Put the grinds into the damp filter. Zero out the weight and start the timer. In a clockwise motion, pour in 50 grams of water to bloom the coffee grinds. Let the water filter through the grinds for 30 seconds. Slowly add more water until the scale reads 340 grams; this should take about 4 minutes. Remove the filter and discard. Pour the coffee into a mug and enjoy.

HERE'S HOW I DRINK IT: Warm and black.

BLACK AND WHITE RUSSIAN

SERVES 4

Boozy coffee topped with vanilla whipped cream is a signal to the brain that it's time to "wake up!" and "take it easy!" It's a balance that we want to be alert enough to enjoy. This lightly sweetened spiked coffee is extra decadent when topped with lightly whipped cream. I like to serve this with Coffee Ice Cubes (page 39) and layer the whipped cream on top, stirring just slightly and allowing the drink to become more milky with time. I love this drink served with Sweet Bacon Pancakes (page 91).

½ cup plus 3 tablespoons sugar

½ cup water

3 cups strong coffee, chilled

4 ounces Kahlúa

2 ounces vodka

½ of a vanilla bean, seeds scraped

1½ cups heavy cream

Ice or Coffee Ice Cubes (page 39), for serving

1. In a small saucepan set over medium heat, combine the ½ cup of sugar and water. Cook, stirring, about 4 minutes, until the sugar dissolves. Let the simple syrup cool completely before using.

2. In a large measuring cup, stir together the simple syrup, coffee, Kahlúa, and vodka. Refrigerate until ready to assemble the drinks.

3. In a small bowl, combine the 3 tablespoons of sugar and the vanilla bean seeds. Using your fingers or the back of a spoon, crush any clumps to disperse the vanilla beans throughout the sugar.

4. In the bowl of an electric mixer fitted with a whisk attachment, or using an electric hand mixer, beat the cream and vanilla sugar on medium speed for about 6 minutes, until it holds soft peaks. This won't be firm whipped cream, but rather, very soft and light.

5. To serve, fill four small glasses with ice. Fill each glass two-thirds full with the coffee mixture. Top each with the whipped cream, and serve.

EGGS

In my family, you can eat eggs one of two ways: the Sunday soft-boil or not at all. I remember busy Sunday mornings getting ready for church. While I was unceremoniously scratching at my church tights and loathing my dress shoes, my mom would hand my sister and me a plate with her signature soft-boiled egg and a mostly toasted slice of wheat bread. At that age, I always felt that the best expression of an egg was in a chocolate chip cookie, not in a soft, white, goopy center that, if you're asking me, tasted nothing like a Cadbury Creme Egg as I had hoped it would. It took me nearly a lifetime to enjoy a runny egg yolk, but now I know without a doubt that the egg (runny or stiff) is the perfect food.

A good egg—thoughtfully prepared, hard fried or easy poached—is the backbone of any good brunch table. Brunch is when you want to show off your ability to tame an egg white but still coax a gorgeous runny yolk from its center. I'm here to foster those skills.

The recipes in this chapter celebrate the flexibility and beauty of the egg. Now that I appreciate the real deal over relegating them to cookies (though I'm certain that's not a terrible move), I'm in awe of the many ways we can enjoy them. These recipes aim to be as versatile as eggs themselves so that you have an arsenal of egg dishes to treat just yourself on a weekend morning or impress a large group of hungry brunchers. I've also included some of my best-egg secrets. From cooking with ghee, spritzing with lime, and straining egg whites, I'm sharing all of my egg-hacks in the hope that your brunch table shines bright with runny yolks and smiling faces.

THE SECRET TO
FLUFFY SCRAMBLED EGGS

SERVES 1

Telling someone how to scramble eggs might be a bit like writing a recipe for boiling water. Eggs + pan + heat = rather fine scrambled eggs, no matter what you do to them. Fine eggs are one thing, but great eggs are slightly more elusive. There are some tricks, from seasoning to heating and stirring, that make all the difference. I consider very good scrambled eggs an important life skill. Great eggs are that serious.

3 large eggs

2 tablespoons whole milk

½ teaspoon soy sauce

I tablespoon Clarified Butter
 (recipe follows)

Small squeeze of fresh lime juice

Freshly cracked black pepper

1. In a medium bowl, whisk together the eggs, milk, and soy sauce.

2. In a nonstick skillet set over medium-low heat, melt the clarified butter, swirling the pan to coat it evenly. Add the eggs to the hot pan and let them sit for 10 seconds. Using a rubber spatula, push and flip the eggs around the pan, stirring constantly, for 4 to 5 minutes, until the eggs are just cooked through. Squeeze with a bit of fresh lime just before the eggs finish cooking. Transfer to a plate, season with pepper, and serve warm.

TIPS FOR GREAT SCRAMBLED EGGS

• Using a whisk to beat the eggs with the milk and soy sauce will ensure that the egg whites are well broken down and aerated.

• Milk will add a light creaminess. For more richness, substitute heavy cream for the milk.

• I find that soy sauce adds not only saltiness but also a fantastic savory quality, and the liquid evenly disperses throughout the eggs.

HOW TO MAKE CLARIFIED BUTTER

MAKES ABOUT 1¾ CUPS

The recipes in this chapter call for clarified butter. Clarified butter is pure butterfat, which results when the milk solids and water have been separated from the butterfat. Clarified butter is a game changer when it comes to cooking eggs because it can withstand high heat without burning, since it no longer contains the elements that can brown and eventually burn (milk solids). While browned butter (made by cooking butter until the milk solids caramelize; see page 97) is delicious in our baked treats, it's much harder to control in a frying pan with eggs. Clarified butter enables us to create delicious and consistent butter-fried eggs.

1. Set the strainer in the bowl and line it with two layers of cheesecloth.

2. Cut the butter into small cubes. In a medium saucepan set over medium-low heat, melt the butter for about 4 minutes. It will begin to spit and crackle as it heats; that's the water cooking out of the butter. Foam will form on the top as it simmers; use a spoon to carefully scoop away as much of the foam as you can. Continue to heat the butter until brown bits form on the bottom of the pan. At this stage, the butter will be nutty and fragrant.

3. Remove the pan from the heat and immediately pour the butter through the cheesecloth-lined strainer and into the bowl. Discard the cheesecloth and stir a few pinches of sea salt into the clarified butter. Let cool to room temperature. Clarified butter will keep for up to 3 months in an airtight container in the refrigerator or at room temperature.

SPECIAL EQUIPMENT
Fine-mesh strainer
Cheesecloth

1 pound good-quality unsalted butter
Sea salt

THE SECRET TO
GREAT FRIED EGGS

MAKES 2 FRIED EGGS; SERVES 1

Fried eggs are simple. Get a pan hot enough, add some fat, send an egg crashing in, and a few minutes later, our egg has turned into breakfast. As with every egg endeavor, very good fried eggs take some time to finesse. Here is my go-to method to fried egg bliss and ways to modify based on your preferences.

Melt the butter in a nonstick pan set over medium heat. Crack the eggs into the pan. Season with salt and pepper. Cook for about 3 minutes, until the egg whites just begin to set. Carefully flip the egg and cook to desired yolk doneness (about 4 minutes for medium).

l tablespoon Clarified Butter
(page 57)

2 large eggs

Salt

Freshly cracked black pepper

TIPS FOR GREAT FRIED EGGS

- Before placing eggs in the pan to fry, first crack the eggs into a fine-mesh strainer. This will strain the watery portion of the egg white, leaving the more firm white surrounding the yolk, which creates a neater, more compact fried egg.

- For a delicate fried egg, once you have the eggs in the pan and seasoned, add 1 teaspoon water to the pan and immediately cover with a lid. As the eggs cook, they will steam. Cook until the egg whites are set and the yolks are to the desired doneness, about 3 minutes for over easy.

- For a crisper egg, once you flip the eggs, use the spatula to press down on the edges of the egg as it cooks, which will create a crisp egg-white edge. Cook to the desired doneness, about 3 minutes for over easy.

- For a richer fried egg, try basting it in butter as it cooks. Increase the butter amount to 2 tablespoons, and spoon hot butter over the top as the egg cooks.

THE SECRET TO
VERY EASY POACHED EGGS

SERVES 2

There are exactly 5,983 ways to poach an egg—which is strange, considering we're just boiling an egg out of its shell. Some say you need a dash of vinegar, others argue you need a special flip of the wrist to create a vortex in the water at the exact moment the eggs are dropped into the simmering water. Any breakfast recipe that requires a vortex is automatically too complicated for me. It'll never happen while I'm simultaneously clutching a Bloody Mary, trying not to forget the toast in the oven, and welcoming guests to the brunch table. Instead, I have the following method for poaching eggs, without the madness.

1. Crack an egg into the strainer and shake lightly, allowing the looser, more watery egg white to strain off.

2. Bring a large saucepan of water to a light simmer. Place one egg in the strainer and gently lower the strainer into the simmering water. Tilt and shake the strainer lightly to coax the egg out of the strainer and into the boiling water. Swirl the water lightly with a spatula. Add up to three more eggs, simmering and lightly stirring, for 3 to 4 minutes, until the whites are firm throughout. Remove the eggs from the simmering water and serve warm.

SPECIAL EQUIPMENT
Fine-mesh strainer

4 large eggs

- Make sure your eggs are as fresh as possible. To test the freshness, place an egg in a measuring cup of water so that the water covers the egg. If the egg stands upright or floats, it's old. If the egg lies on its side on the bottom of the measuring cup, it's fresh.

- Straining the egg will create a tighter, neater egg white around the yolk.

- You can strain eggs ahead of time, placing them in small bowls until you're ready to poach them.

- You can poach eggs ahead of time and leave them to rest in a bowl of cool water in the refrigerator overnight. Place eggs in a bowl of warm water for about 20 minutes before serving.

THE SECRET TO
PERFECTLY BOILED EGGS

MAKES 12 BOILED EGGS

It's far too easy to overboil an egg if you don't know the right technique. You only need one foolproof method, and this is the one that works perfectly for me every time. It's easy to remember, and you won't end up with that gray ring (from overcooking) around the yolk.

1. Fill a medium saucepan with cold water. Put the pan over medium-high heat and bring the water to a rolling boil (not a simmer or a light boil but a full-on, take-no-prisoners boil).

2. Remove the eggs from the refrigerator; wait until the last second to pull them out. Using a large spoon, gently lower the cold eggs into the boiling water. Reduce the heat to medium and boil the eggs until they've reach the desired doneness, 8 minutes for soft-boiled and 11 minutes for hard-boiled.

3. Remove the pan from the heat and drain. Fill the pan with cool tap water and add a handful of ice cubes to stop the cooking process. Let the eggs rest for about 5 minutes, until they are cool enough to handle, and then peel.

12 large eggs, cold

TIPS FOR GREAT BOILED EGGS

• Cook 8 minutes for a soft-boiled egg.

• Cook 9 to 10 minutes for a soft-boiled egg that's just slightly more cooked through.

• Cook 11 minutes for a perfectly hard-boiled egg.

• Try not to drop the eggs into the boiling water, or they will crack and the egg insides will boil out.

• If you're afraid that the cold eggs will explode in the boiling water, don't be. This rarely happens—eggshells are resilient!

• To easily and neatly peel the eggs, crack them in the ice water, allowing the water to seep between the cooked egg and the shell membrane. Peel, leaving the peels behind in the pan.

BROCCOLI AND CHEDDAR QUICHE

SERVES 6 TO 8

This broccoli-loaded quiche is a super-versatile dish that can morph from a delicious breakfast served with Praline Bacon (page 130) to a satisfying late lunch served with a simple green salad. It's a crowd-pleaser, thanks in large part to a simple puff pastry crust and loads of melt-y cheddar cheese. (See photograph, page 52.)

1. Place a rack in the center of the oven and preheat the oven to 375°F.

2. On a lightly floured work surface, unfold the puff pastry. Using a floured rolling pin, gently roll out the puff pastry, increasing the top and bottom edges by about an inch to create a square. Transfer to a 9-inch pie dish; roll the edges under, if necessary. Let rest in the refrigerator while you make the filling.

3. In a large sauté pan set over medium heat, heat the oil. Add the onions and cook, stirring, 4 to 6 minutes, until translucent and just starting to brown. Add the broccoli and toss gently, for about 3 minutes, until bright green and just beginning to soften. Add 2 tablespoons of water to the pan. Cover with a tight-fitting lid on the pan and steam the broccoli with the onions for 2 minutes, until crisp-tender. Uncover, remove the pan from the heat, and let cool until room temperature, about 20 minutes.

4. In a large bowl, whisk together the eggs, milk, half-and-half, salt, pepper, and nutmeg. Gently stir in the cheese. Add the cooled broccoli mixture and stir until thoroughly combined. Pour the filling into the pastry-lined pie dish and smooth the top.

5. Bake for 40 to 45 minutes, until puffed and firm, checking toward the end to ensure that the crust doesn't brown too much on the edges. Let cool for 30 minutes before serving. The quiche can be served warm, at room temperature, or chilled.

All-purpose flour, for rolling

1 sheet all-butter puff pastry, thawed but chilled

2 tablespoons canola oil

1 medium onion, finely chopped

3 heaping cups bite-size broccoli florets

6 large eggs

½ cup whole milk

½ cup half-and-half

¾ teaspoon sea salt

½ teaspoon freshly cracked black pepper

Pinch of freshly grated nutmeg

1 cup grated sharp cheddar cheese

THE SECRET TO
ANYTHING SKILLET HASH

SERVES 4

When a big ol' brunch can come from one cast-iron skillet, it's fair to say we're doing things right. When that same skillet breakfast also helps us clean leftovers out of the refrigerator, we're really on to something great! Here's how to pull together a one-skillet brunch hash with dang-near whatever you have in the refrigerator.

1. In a large cast-iron skillet, at least 10 inches, add a few tablespoons of canola oil or clarified butter and heat over medium heat.

2. A good breakfast hash is all about layering. Add your meat: bacon, Italian sausage, turkey kielbasa, last night's pork shoulder, or whatever you have on hand that sounds good. Cook the meat until either cooked through or browned well, depending on whether it was raw to start. Transfer to a plate. Leave all of the delicious fat in the pan, and keep the pan over medium heat.

3. Add your vegetables: onions, bell pepper, and potatoes are a great place to start. Chop all the vegetables into ½-inch dice so they cook evenly. Cook, stirring occasionally, usually around 8 to 10 minutes, until cooked through. (If using potatoes, place a lid on the pan to help them cook faster.) Other delicious additions are sweet potatoes, sliced carrots, and sliced mushrooms.

4. Next, add your optional vegetables. Cook, tossing the mixture together, for about 4 minutes, until lightly browned and warmed through. Return the meat to the pan and toss.

5. Make places for the eggs by creating four wells in the hash mixture, scooping it aside; you want the eggs to touch the bottom of the pan. Add the eggs, season with salt and pepper, and cover. Cook for about 5 to 7 minutes, until the egg whites are set.

6. Remove the pan from the heat and add any toppings. Serve warm.

Canola oil or Clarified Butter (page 57)

BREAKFAST MEAT

6 slices bacon or 2 uncooked Italian sausage links, 2 heaping cups sliced turkey kielbasa, I heaping cup roasted pork shoulder . . .

VEGETABLES

I medium onion, chopped; ½ bell pepper, chopped; 2 medium russet or sweet potatoes, chopped; I cup sliced carrots; I heaping cup sliced cremini mushrooms . . .

OPTIONAL VEGETABLES

I cup fresh corn, I cup thawed peas, handful of chopped kale, handful of fresh spinach . . .

EGGS

4 large eggs

Salt

Freshly cracked black pepper

TOPPINGS

Fresh parsley, fresh chives, grated cheddar cheese, crumbled feta cheese, hot sauce . . .

BACON AND DEVILED EGGS

MAKES 24 DEVILED EGGS

No matter how many deviled eggs I make for a brunch gathering, they always seem to disappear in no time. Never mind the fact that I've been known to position myself next to the platter of deviled eggs and pop them in one bite when no one is looking. They're kitschy, classic, and irresistible. Add bacon, and they're extra perfect for brunch.

1. Fill a large pot with water about 5 inches high and bring the water to a rolling boil over medium heat. Take the eggs out of the refrigerator just as the water boils. Using a large spoon, lower the eggs into the boiling water. After a few eggs, the water will cool and stop boiling. That's okay. Once the last egg is in, cook them for 11 to 12 minutes, occasionally stirring gently. Use the spoon to transfer the eggs to a large bowl filled with ice water. Let cool for 5 minutes.

2. Peel the eggs, rinse off any shell bits, and pat them dry. Slice the eggs in half the long way and carefully spoon the yolks into a medium bowl (if you're mixing by hand) or the bowl of a food processor fitted with the regular chopping blade (if you're mixing in a machine). Place the egg white halves on a serving platter.

3. To the egg yolks, add the mayonnaise and both mustards. Mash and stir with a fork or blend until smooth in a food processor. If using a processor, transfer the mixture now to a medium bowl. Stir in the Worcestershire sauce, chives, and bacon bits. Season to taste with salt and pepper.

4. Spoon about 2 heaping teaspoons into each egg white. Top with more chives, bacon, dill, thinly sliced radish, and a sprinkling of paprika just before serving. The eggs are best within 2 days of preparing. Serve chilled.

12 large eggs

½ cup mayonnaise

2 teaspoons Dijon or whole-grain mustard

2 teaspoons yellow mustard

½ teaspoon Worcestershire sauce

3 tablespoons chopped fresh chives, plus 1 tablespoon for garnish

3 tablespoons finely chopped cooked bacon, plus 1 tablespoon more for garnish

Salt

Freshly cracked black pepper

GARNISHES

Fresh dill, lightly chopped

Thinly sliced radishes

Paprika

CAJUN SOUFFLÉ

SERVES 6

I've learned a thing or two about New Orleans cooking. I've learned enough to know that, as a Californian and not a native New Orleanian, I'm not really allowed to call any of my cooking Cajun. I've eaten too many avocados and not enough crawfish in my life to call anything Cajun. Luckily, I'm not listening. I've combined the trinity—bell pepper, onion, and parsley—with creole seasoning, and I made this in my kitchen in New Orleans. So, dangit . . . it's Cajun!

1. Place a rack in the center of the oven and preheat the oven to 350°F. Generously butter a 2-quart baking dish and set aside.

2. In a medium skillet set over medium heat, heat the oil. Add the onions and bell pepper. Cook 5 to 7 minutes, stirring, until soft, translucent, and lightly browned. Add the garlic and parsley and cook for 1 minute. Stir in the creole seasoning, cumin, and black pepper. Reduce the heat to low, sprinkle in the flour, and stir. Slowly whisk in the milk. Cook, whisking constantly, 6 to 8 minutes, until thick and bubbling. Add the sausage and stir.

3. Separate the eggs and place the egg yolks in a medium bowl. Place the egg whites in the bowl of a stand mixer fitted with the whisk attachment. Whisk the egg yolks until well combined. Add about ½ cup of the vegetable mixture to the egg yolks and whisk well.

4. Beat the egg whites on medium speed. When they begin to foam, add the salt and cream of tartar. Increase the speed slightly and beat for 5 to 6 minutes, until soft peaks form. Spoon about a third of the egg whites into the egg yolk mixture. Fold until just combined. Add another third of the egg whites and fold to combine. Add the final third and fold until combined. Spoon into the prepared pan.

5. Bake 40 to 45 minutes, until puffed, browned, and no longer jiggling in the center. Let cool for 15 minutes; serve warm.

Unsalted butter, for the baking dish

2 tablespoons canola oil

⅓ cup finely chopped yellow onion

⅓ cup finely chopped green bell pepper

1 garlic clove, minced

2 tablespoons chopped fresh parsley

2 teaspoons creole seasoning with salt (I like Tony Chachere's)

½ teaspoon ground cumin

½ teaspoon freshly cracked black pepper

¼ cup all-purpose flour

1¾ cups whole milk, at room temperature

1 heaping cup chopped cooked Andouille sausage

6 large eggs, separated

Pinch of salt

Pinch of cream of tartar

ONION, GRUYÈRE, AND GRITS
FRITTATA MUFFINS

MAKES 12 MUFFINS

A magical thing happens when you combine butter, onions, and a good, long time in the skillet. Deeply browned and caramelized onions emerge with an irresistible sweetness and underlying savory qualities. Here I've combined onions with salty, cheesy grits and creamy whipped eggs for compact all-in-one breakfast bites.

1. **FOR THE GRITS:** In a medium saucepan set over medium heat, bring the water to a boil. Add the salt and, stirring constantly, slowly mix in the grits. Reduce the heat to low and cook, stirring constantly, 2 to 3 minutes longer than the package instructions. The grits will be thick. Remove the pan from the heat and stir in the cheese and pepper. Let cool.

2. **FOR THE ONIONS:** In a medium skillet set over medium heat, melt the butter with the oil. Add the onions and stir to coat in the fat. Let cook, undisturbed, for about 4 minutes. Add the sugar, salt, pepper, and thyme and stir. Cook, undisturbed, in 4-minute increments until the onions have browned and resemble jam, about 12 minutes total. Lower the heat if the onions brown too quickly.

3. **FOR THE EGG MIXTURE:** In a medium bowl, whisk together the eggs, cream, salt, and pepper.

4. Grease a 12-cup muffin tin with butter. Add a heaping spoonful of grits to each cup and divide the onions between the cups. Top each with eggs, filling to just over three-quarters full.

5. Bake for 20 to 22 minutes, until puffed, browned, and cooked through. Let cool for 10 minutes before running a butter knife around each muffin and removing them from the pan. Sprinkle with chopped chives and enjoy them warm!

GRITS
2 cups water

¼ teaspoon salt

½ cup finely ground yellow grits

⅓ cup grated Gruyère cheese

½ teaspoon freshly cracked black pepper

ONIONS
2 tablespoons unsalted butter

1 tablespoon canola oil

2 medium onions, cut in half and into medium slices

Pinch of sugar

Salt

Freshly cracked black pepper

½ teaspoon fresh thyme leaves

EGG MIXTURE
6 large eggs

¾ cup heavy cream

½ teaspoon salt

½ teaspoon freshly cracked black pepper

2 tablespoons unsalted butter, softened, for greasing the pan

2 tablespoons fresh chopped chives, for garnish

SPAGHETTI QUICHE

SERVES 6 TO 8

Let's count all the times I've stood in front of an open refrigerator door eating cold spaghetti from last night's dinner. I don't have enough fingers to count. To make spaghetti officially brunchable, I've made it part of a creamy, crustless quiche. With a side of Spicy Brown Sugar Sausage Patties (page 135), and plenty of Grapefruit-Rosemary Mimosas (page 23), you have a supremely tasty meal. The quiche is delicious served warm and cool. (See photograph, page 6.)

1. Place a rack in the center of the oven and preheat to 375°F. Generously brush a 10-inch oven-safe skillet or 10-inch pie dish with butter and set aside.

2. FOR THE SPAGHETTI: Cook the pasta al dente, according to the package instructions. Drain and return to the pot. Add 1 tablespoon butter and stir until melted. Add the marinara sauce and cheese, and stir well. Transfer to the prepared baking dish, without packing it down too much.

3. FOR THE QUICHE: In a medium bowl, whisk together the eggs, cream, milk, butter, basil, salt, and pepper. Pour the mixture over the spaghetti.

4. Bake 30 to 35 minutes, until the quiche is set and no longer jiggling. Turn on the oven broiler and heat the quiche under the broiler up to 5 minutes, until the top is golden. Let stand for 15 minutes. Sprinkle with basil before serving. This quiche is delicious served warm, at room temperature, or chilled.

SPAGHETTI

1 tablespoon unsalted butter, plus more for the baking dish

1 pound spaghetti

2 cups jarred marinara sauce

½ cup grated Parmesan cheese

QUICHE

6 large eggs

½ cup heavy cream

½ cup whole milk

3 tablespoons unsalted butter, melted

¼ cup coarsely chopped fresh basil, plus more for garnish

1½ teaspoons salt

¾ teaspoon freshly cracked black pepper

EGG WHITE OMELET
WITH CARAMELIZED MUSHROOMS AND HERBS

SERVES 1

I enjoy egg-white omelets, not because of their pure protein health benefits, but because I genuinely enjoy the taste of egg whites. When cooked in an omelet, they take on a buttery quality. Filled with savory mushrooms, a hint of cheese, and bright herbs, this breakfast is completely satisfying, and the healthfulness is just a bonus! This recipe makes just one omelet, but it scales up nicely for a group.

1. **FOR THE MUSHROOMS:** In a medium nonstick skillet set over medium heat, melt the butter. Add the mushrooms, toss to coat in the butter, and season with salt and pepper. Cook 8 to 10 minutes, stirring occasionally, until browned. If the mushrooms begin to burn, reduce the heat to low. Drizzle with vinegar, stir, and transfer to a small plate.

2. **FOR THE OMELET:** In a small bowl, whisk the egg whites and soy sauce for about 3 minutes by hand, until frothy.

3. Clean and dry the skillet, and set it over medium-low heat. Melt the butter in the pan. Add the egg whites and shake the pan so that they cover the bottom. Use a rubber spatula to lift the edges of the cooked egg and tilt the pan so that the uncooked parts seep underneath and cook. Cook for about 5 minutes, until the top just begins to set.

4. Remove the pan from the heat. Spoon the mushrooms over half of the egg whites, sprinkle with the cheese and herbs, and fold the other half of the egg whites over the filling. Shimmy the omelet onto a plate and enjoy.

MUSHROOMS

1 tablespoon Clarified Butter (page 57)

1½ cups sliced cremini mushrooms

Sea salt

Freshly cracked black pepper

Splash of balsamic vinegar

OMELET

4 large egg whites

Splash of soy sauce or tamari

1 tablespoon Clarified Butter (page 57)

3 tablespoons freshly grated Parmesan cheese

2 tablespoons chopped fresh tarragon and parsley

EXTRA-EGG-AND-BACON
FRIED RICE

SERVES 4

Slide the potatoes aside. I took this ultra-comforting Chinese take-out dish and made it breakfast-friendly with bacon and loads of eggs. It's best and easiest to make this with leftover rice (from Friday night's Chinese food, clearly). If you happen to have leftovers, this dish lasts well in the refrigerator and can be reheated with another dash of soy sauce to moisten.

8 slices bacon

3 tablespoons sesame oil

⅓ cup sliced scallions (both white and green parts), plus more for garnish

½ cup frozen peas, thawed

6 cups cooked white rice

3 tablespoons soy sauce, plus more to taste

2 tablespoons rice vinegar

1 to 2 tablespoon Sriracha or your favorite hot sauce

2 large eggs, beaten

4 large fried eggs (see page 58)

1 ripe avocado, sliced (optional)

1. Place a rack in the upper third of the oven and preheat the oven to 375°F.

2. Line a rimmed baking sheet with foil. Arrange the bacon in a single layer on the pan. Bake for 17 to 20 minutes, until cooked through and crisp. Let cool, and then chop.

3. In a large skillet set over medium heat, heat the sesame oil. Add the scallions and peas and cook, stirring, until the scallions are softened and the peas are warmed through, about 3 minutes. Add the cooked rice and toss to combine, breaking up any clumps. Let the veggies and rice cook about 6 minutes, until slightly browned.

4. In a small bowl, stir together the soy sauce, rice vinegar, and hot sauce. Pour the mixture over the fried rice. Add the chopped bacon and stir well. Scrape the rice to one side of the pan and pour the eggs into the other side of the pan. Stir immediately to scramble the eggs as they cook. As the eggs begin to firm up, stir the rice into the eggs. Taste and season with more soy sauce and/or hot sauce, as desired.

5. To serve, divide the rice among four shallow bowls. Top each with a fried egg, and divide the avocado (if using) and chopped scallions among the bowls.

HUEVOS RANCHEROS
WITH ELOTE TOPPING

SERVES 6

Huevos rancheros—the combination of soft fried corn tortillas and eggs—is very simple, and very delicious. I've amped it up a bit by adding smoky chipotle peppers to a tomato-based sauce and a spicy topping of sweet corn. It makes for a very satisfying late morning meal. I find that a bold and spicy egg dish is just the ticket after a night of boozy overindulgence. While we're at it, maybe a little hair of the dog is in order; I recommend a Peach and Orange Paloma (page 15).

1. **FOR THE TOMATO SAUCE:** In a medium saucepan set over medium heat, heat the canola oil. Add the onions and cook, stirring, for about 5 minutes, until softened. Add the garlic and cook, stirring, for 1 minute. Add the oregano, salt, and pepper and cook for 2 minutes, until just fragrant. Add the tomatoes, chipotle peppers, and adobo sauce, and cook for 10 minutes, until thickened slightly, using a wooden spoon to break up the tomatoes and peppers.

2. **FOR THE ELOTE:** In a medium bowl, combine the corn, cheese, olive oil, mayonnaise, cilantro, jalapeño, salt, and pepper.

3. In a medium skillet set over medium heat, heat 2 tablespoons of the canola oil. Fry the tortillas, flipping once, until soft, about 3 minutes. Transfer to paper towels to drain. Add another tablespoon or two of oil to the pan to fry all of the tortillas.

4. Heat the remaining 5 tablespoons oil in the pan and fry the eggs until set, about 2 minutes. Flip the eggs once if you'd like them more cooked. For a softer yolk, don't flip, and cover the pan.

5. Place two tortillas on each of six plates. Top each tortilla with a spoonful of sauce and a fried egg. Divide the elote mixture among the tortillas, followed by the avocado and a wedge of lime.

TOMATO SAUCE
1 tablespoon canola oil
1/3 cup chopped yellow onion
1 garlic clove, minced
Scant 1 teaspoon dried oregano
Salt
Freshly cracked black pepper
1 (14-ounce) can crushed tomatoes
2 whole chipotle peppers in adobo sauce, plus 3 tablespoons adobo sauce

ELOTE
Kernels from 4 ears fresh corn
1/2 cup cojita cheese, crumbled
2 tablespoons olive oil
1 tablespoon mayonnaise
3 tablespoons chopped fresh cilantro leaves
2 tablespoons finely chopped jalapeño, seeded
Salt
Freshly cracked black pepper

About 1/2 cup canola oil
12 corn tortillas
12 large eggs
1 ripe avocado, sliced, for serving
6 wedges of lime, for serving

PEA AND GOAT CHEESE
TORTILLA

SERVES 6 TO 8

The classic Spanish tortilla is a baked mixture of eggs and potatoes, sort of like a crustless quiche loaded with layers of soft potato slices. I added green peas and tangy goat cheese, making it a really beautiful dish for a spring morning. No need for an extra side of hash browns, but a side of Spicy Brown Sugar Sausage Patties (page 135) would be exceptional.

5 tablespoons canola oil

I small yellow onion, cut in half and into medium slices

3 large russet potatoes, peeled and sliced ⅛-inch thick

3 tablespoons Clarified Butter (page 57)

Kosher salt

Freshly cracked black pepper

8 large eggs

2 tablespoons finely chopped flat-leaf parsley

¼ cup heavy cream

I cup frozen peas, thawed

⅔ cup crumbled goat cheese

1. Place a rack in the middle of the oven and preheat to 400°F. Line a rimmed baking sheet with foil and set aside.

2. In a medium sauté pan set over medium heat, heat 2 tablespoons of the oil. Add the onions and cook, stirring, for 6 minutes, until translucent and just starting to brown. Add 3 tablespoons of water and cook for about 4 minutes, scraping up any brown bits from the bottom of the pan, until the water evaporates and the onions take on a uniform brown color.

3. Transfer the onions to the prepared roasting pan. Add the potato slices and toss well. Add 1 tablespoon of the butter and the remaining 3 tablespoons oil, and season generously with salt and pepper. Toss with tongs. Cover the pan with foil.

4. Bake until the potatoes are tender, 25 to 30 minutes. Let cool for 15 minutes. Reduce the oven temperature to 350°F.

5. In a medium bowl, whisk together the eggs, parsley, and cream. Stir in the peas and half of the goat cheese. Season with salt and pepper.

6. In a 10-inch cast-iron skillet set over medium-high heat, melt the remaining 2 tablespoons butter, swirling the pan so that the butter coats the sides of the pan as well. Add half of the cooked

potatoes and goat cheese to the pan. Top with half of the egg mixture, spreading the peas as evenly as possible across the pan. Add the remaining potatoes, followed by the remaining egg mixture, again spreading the remaining peas and goat cheese across the tortilla. Cover with foil.

7. Bake for 30 minutes. Remove the foil and bake for 5 to 10 more minutes, until the tortilla is slightly browned and lightly puffed. Slice and serve directly from the skillet, warm, or at room temperature.

BAKED RATATOUILLE HASH
WITH FRIED EGGS

SERVES 6

It's beautiful the way tomato, zucchini, eggplant, and bell peppers come together. It feels ancient and comforting, like grandmothers of grandmothers once stirred together this same mixture on their stovetops forever ago. This breakfast hash is a riff on a traditional Provençal vegetable stew. To simplify the ratatouille, I roast the vegetables all at once in the oven until browned and softened. Topped with fried eggs and fresh basil, this hash is a fresh, summertime alternative to a potato-based hash.

I pint cherry tomatoes, halved

2 medium zucchini, cut into medium chunks

I medium eggplant, cut into medium chunks

I large yellow onion, cut into medium chunks

I red bell pepper, seeded and cut into medium chunks

3 garlic cloves, crushed

¼ cup olive oil

I teaspoon crushed red pepper flakes

Sea salt

4 tablespoons Clarified Butter (page 57)

6 large eggs

¼ cup coarsely chopped fresh basil

6 slices of sourdough toast, for serving

1. Place a rack in the center and another in the upper third of the oven and preheat to 400°F. Line two rimmed baking sheets with parchment paper and set aside.

2. Place the tomatoes, zucchini, eggplant, onions, bell pepper, and garlic in a large bowl. Add the olive oil, red pepper flakes, and salt, and toss well. Spread the vegetables in an even layer on the prepared baking sheets.

3. Roast for 35 to 45 minutes, stirring every 15 minutes, until softened and browned. Let cool slightly.

4. In a nonstick skillet set over medium heat, melt 1 tablespoon of the butter. Crack 2 eggs into the pan and season with salt and pepper. Cover the pan and cook for about 4 minutes, until the whites are set and the yolks have just begun to set. Transfer to a plate. Repeat with the remaining eggs, adding more butter to the pan as necessary.

5. To serve, spoon the roasted vegetables onto six plates. Top with a fried egg. Sprinkle with fresh basil and serve with a slice of toast.

SHAKSHUKA
WITH FETA AND PARSLEY

MAKES 4 LARGER OR 6 SMALL SERVINGS

Shakshuka is easily my favorite egg recipe I discovered in brunch-bingeing my way (for research, of course) through the last year. I found it after wandering into an Israeli coffee shop in Philadelphia, having just attended a Quaker meeting for Easter. It was an eclectic day, to say the least. In the café were crowded tables of happy diners, enjoying sizzling skillets of spiced tomato and poached egg. Incredible for the smell alone, the taste is just as spicy and rich. A crusty piece of bread is a must for sopping up the sauce.

1. Place a rack in the center of the oven and preheat the oven to 375°F.

2. In a 10-inch oven-safe skillet set over medium heat, heat the oil and butter until the butter melts. Add the onions and bell pepper and cook for 10 to 12 minutes, stirring, until the vegetables are very soft. Stir in the garlic and cook for another 2 minutes. Add the cumin, sweet paprika, smoked paprika, cayenne pepper, and oregano and stir well.

3. Add the tomatoes and use the back of a spoon to break up the tomatoes. Stir in the salt and pepper and simmer gently for 8 to 10 minutes, until the sauce is bubbling and slightly thickened. Remove the pan from the heat. Add ½ cup of the feta and stir. Crack the eggs into the tomato mixture and use the spoon to gently nestle the eggs in the sauce. Season the eggs with salt and pepper.

4. Bake for 10 minutes, until the egg whites are set. Let cool for 5 minutes. Sprinkle with parsley and the remaining ½ cup feta. Serve warm with the pita bread.

2 tablespoons olive oil

1 tablespoon Clarified Butter (page 57)

1 medium onion, chopped

1 red bell pepper, seeded, and finely chopped

2 garlic cloves, thinly sliced

1 teaspoon ground cumin

1 teaspoon sweet paprika

½ teaspoon smoked paprika

¼ teaspoon cayenne pepper

¼ teaspoon dried oregano

1 (28-ounce) can whole tomatoes, broken up with the back of a spoon

Salt

Freshly cracked black pepper

1 cup crumbled feta cheese

6 large eggs

¼ cup coarsely chopped parsley, for garnish

4 warm pita breads, cut into wedges, for serving

SHRIMP AND GRITS
WITH POACHED EGGS

SERVES 4

Shrimp and Grits is a traditional Southern breakfast in which gulf shrimp, sausage, and plenty of butter are celebrated with abandon. This version is straightforward, featuring creamy, cheesy grits topped with crumbled Italian sausage, lemon shrimp, and poached eggs. Serve this traditional Southern brunch with Grapefruit Rosemary Mimosas (page 23) and a slight drawl in your speech.

1. In a saucepan set over high heat, bring the water to a boil. Whisking constantly, gradually add the grits to the water. Add a pinch of salt and pepper. Reduce the heat to low, bring to a simmer, and cook, covered, according to the package directions, until the water is absorbed.

2. Remove the pan from the heat and stir in the cream, butter, and cheese.

3. In a medium skillet set over medium heat, cook the sausage, breaking up any lumps with the back of a spoon, for about 8 minutes, until it is cooked through. Add the garlic and cook for 1 more minute. Add the shrimp and cook for about 6 minutes, until the shrimp turn pink. Add the lemon juice, scallions, and parsley. Cook for 3 minutes, until warmed through.

4. Spoon the grits into four serving bowls. Top each with some shrimp and sausage mixture. Finish each bowl with a poached egg on top, and serve warm.

4 cups water

I cup stone-ground grits

Salt

Freshly cracked black pepper

½ cup heavy cream

3 tablespoons unsalted butter

I cup shredded sharp cheddar cheese

½ pound spicy Italian sausage, casings removed

I large garlic clove, minced

I pound shrimp, peeled and deveined, tails removed

4 teaspoons fresh lemon juice

½ cup thinly sliced scallions (both white and green parts)

2 tablespoons chopped fresh parsley

4 poached eggs (see page 60)

SPINACH AND ARTICHOKE
OMELET WHEELS

SERVES 4 TO 6

How to make an omelet for many without sweating over the stove while you flip and fold a hundred times? I've hacked the traditional recipe for you (you're welcome). By baking the eggs and toppings in a jelly roll pan, you can then roll it all up into a tight spiral, slice it into portions, and share. It's very easy, and looks pretty fancy, too.

Nonstick cooking spray

¼ cup all-purpose flour

½ cup whole milk

½ cup heavy cream

8 large eggs

2 tablespoons unsalted butter, melted

1 tablespoon whole-grain mustard

1 scant teaspoon soy sauce or tamari

1 scant teaspoon freshly cracked black pepper

1 box frozen spinach, thawed and squeezed of excess water

1 (15-ounce) can artichoke hearts, drained and chopped

2 cups grated Monterey Jack cheese

2 tablespoons chopped chives, for garnish

1. Place a rack in the center of the oven and preheat to 350°F. Coat a 10 × 15-inch jelly roll pan with nonstick cooking spray, line it with parchment paper with an overhang of a few inches on both sides, and lightly spray the parchment paper.

2. Place the flour in a small bowl and slowly pour the milk over the flour. Whisk until smooth. Add the cream and whisk until smooth.

3. In a medium bowl, whisk together the eggs, butter, mustard, soy sauce, and pepper. Add the cream mixture and whisk well by hand for about 3 minutes, until it is fully aerated and has some big bubbles. Pour the mixture into the prepared pan and distribute the spinach, artichoke hearts, and ½ cup of the cheese evenly over the top.

4. Bake for about 12 minutes, until the edges are set and the center is beginning to set. Remove from the oven, sprinkle 1 cup of cheese on top, and bake for 4 to 6 minutes, until the cheese is just melted. Remove the pan from the oven and let cool for 5 minutes.

5. Lift the long end of the parchment paper and tightly roll the omelet to create a long cylinder. Sprinkle with the remaining ½ cup cheese and the chives. Slice and serve!

GRIDDLE

Part of the reason that diner breakfasts are so iconic and delicious is the griddle—that flat-top cook surface on which everything from scrambled eggs to pancakes comes together. This is no accident. There's something very simple and special about cooking on a solid, thick, evenly heated slab of metal. Griddle tops and griddle pans hold memories of delicious breakfasts past and bring that goodness into great brunches going forward. My father has a griddle pan built into the center of his stove, and I'm pretty sure that's where pancakes were born.

You know good things are bound to happen when an entire chapter is named after a pan that makes everything from buttermilk pancakes to grilled cheese sandwiches. If, for whatever reason, you don't have a griddle, perhaps this is just the excuse you need to get one. A good cast-iron skillet will do just fine. A heavy-bottom sauté pan will also do wonderfully. It's not about specific, fancy equipment; brunch is mostly about heart and soul (and really good pancakes).

SWEET BACON PANCAKES

SERVES 6

Full strips of crisp, brown sugar bacon cooked inside of fluffy butter-milk pancakes. If brunching were an Olympic sport—and I'm pretty sure it is—we'd win gold medals across the board in combining two very fine breakfast items into one breakfast-approved cake. Serve alongside Fluffy Scrambled Eggs (page 55) and Frothy, Milky, At-Home Mochas (page 49). (See photograph, page 88.)

1. **FOR THE BACON:** Place racks in the center and upper third of the oven and preheat to 375°F. Line two rimmed baking sheets with foil.

2. Arrange the bacon in single layers on the prepared baking sheets. Sprinkle with the brown sugar and pepper. Bake 15 to 18 minutes, until crisp and sizzling. Transfer the bacon to a plate and let cool slightly. Reduce the oven temperature to 200°F.

3. **FOR THE PANCAKES:** In a medium bowl, whisk together the flour, sugar, baking powder, baking soda, and salt.

4. In a separate medium bowl, whisk together the eggs, butter, buttermilk, and vanilla. Pour the mixture all at once into the flour mixture and whisk well.

5. On a griddle pan or in a nonstick skillet set over medium heat, melt a bit of clarified butter. Spoon ¼-cup portions of the batter into the pan and cook for 1 minute. Press one piece of bacon into each pancake, and continue cooking for about 2 more minutes, until golden brown. Flip the pancakes and cook until the second side is golden brown, 2 to 3 minutes. Transfer the pancakes to an ovenproof plate and keep warm in the oven. Repeat the cooking process with the remaining batter, adding more clarified butter to the pan as necessary.

6. Serve with maple syrup.

BACON

12 thick-cut slices bacon

3 tablespoons lightly packed brown sugar

Freshly cracked black pepper

PANCAKES

2 cups all-purpose flour

2 tablespoons granulated sugar

2 teaspoons baking powder

1 teaspoon baking soda

1 teaspoon salt

2 large eggs

4 tablespoons unsalted butter, melted

2 cups buttermilk

2 teaspoons pure vanilla extract

Clarified Butter (page 57) or canola oil, for the pan

Pure maple syrup, for serving

HAPPY BIRTHDAY PANCAKES

SERVES 1

The existence of a weekend is reason enough to celebrate with decadent brunch, but some brunches are extra special. For those times when a brunch day is also a birthday, these pancakes are a must. Speckled with rainbow sprinkles and made in a small, stackable batch, they're a surprise just for the birthday boy or girl.

1. In a medium bowl, whisk together the flour, granulated sugar, baking powder, baking soda, and salt.

2. In a small bowl, whisk together the egg, buttermilk, butter, and ½ teaspoon of vanilla. Pour the whole mixture into the flour mixture and whisk until the wet and dry ingredients are fully incorporated. Let rest for 10 minutes.

3. In a medium bowl, whisk the cream by hand or with a hand mixer for about 5 minutes, until it holds very soft peaks. Add the confectioners' sugar and a dash of vanilla and beat for about 3 more minutes, until it forms slightly firmer but still spoonable soft peaks.

4. In a medium nonstick skillet over medium heat, melt about half of the clarified butter.

5. Just before cooking the pancakes, fold 2 tablespoons of jimmies into the batter. Spoon 2 heaping tablespoonfuls of batter into the skillet. Cook until browned around the edges, about 2 minutes. Flip the pancake and cook until browned on the other side, about 2 minutes. Transfer to a plate and repeat with the remaining batter, adding the rest of the butter to the pan to cook (you should have 6 small pancakes).

6. Stack all of the pancakes on a plate. Top with the whipped cream, sprinkle with more jimmies, light a candle, and sing "Happy Birthday"!

⅔ cup all-purpose flour

1 tablespoon granulated sugar

½ teaspoon baking powder

½ teaspoon baking soda

Generous pinch of salt

1 large egg

¼ cup buttermilk

1 tablespoon unsalted butter, melted

½ teaspoon plus a dash of pure vanilla extract

½ cup heavy whipping cream

2 teaspoons confectioners' sugar

About 1 tablespoon Clarified Butter (page 57), for the pan

2 tablespoons multicolored jimmies, plus more for topping

THIN OVERNIGHT EGG PANCAKES

MAKES 6 PANCAKES

These thin pancakes are related to crepes but feel less intimidating. The batter comes together quickly and then rests in the refrigerator overnight to thicken just slightly. The next morning, the pancakes are fried in butter and topped with brown sugar and maple syrup. I think they're best enjoyed while leaning against the counter next to the frying pan, folding them up with your fingers. They aren't crepes, so we can forget the formalities.

If you can't find oat flour, you can make your own by processing old-fashioned oats to a fine powder in a spice grinder or a clean coffee grinder. This recipe can be easily doubled to feed many.

¼ cup oat flour

I teaspoon sugar

¼ teaspoon ground cinnamon

Pinch of freshly grated nutmeg

¼ teaspoon salt

2 large eggs

½ cup whole milk

½ teaspoon pure vanilla extract

Clarified Butter (page 57), for the pan

Brown sugar, for serving

Pure maple syrup, for serving

1. In a small bowl, whisk together the oat flour, sugar, cinnamon, nutmeg, and salt.

2. In a medium bowl, whisk together the eggs, milk, and vanilla. Add the oat flour mixture all at once and whisk well. Cover and refrigerate overnight.

3. When ready to cook, remove the batter from the refrigerator and whisk well.

4. In a 6-inch nonstick skillet set over medium-low heat, melt enough clarified butter to lightly coat the bottom of the pan. Spoon 3 tablespoons of batter into the pan, swirling to coat the bottom of the pan. Cook for 3 to 4 minutes, until the top is just set. Using a thin spatula, flip the pancake and cook for 1 minute, until lightly browned on both sides. Transfer the pancake to a plate. Repeat the cooking process with the remaining batter.

5. Sprinkle the pancakes with brown sugar, quickly fold in quarters, and top with maple syrup. Serve warm.

BANANA FRITTERS

SERVES 6

These sweet griddle treats exist in the space between pancakes and fried bananas. They're bready but light, and so packed with bananas that the fruit caramelizes to a golden brown as they fry on the griddle. This is the perfect recipe for that bunch of bananas, bought with the best of intentions, that ends up languishing on the kitchen counter.

1. In a medium bowl, whisk together the flour, brown sugar, baking powder, baking soda, cinnamon, nutmeg, and salt. Set aside.

2. In a separate medium bowl, whisk together the browned butter and the eggs. Whisk in the buttermilk. Pour the mixture all at once into the flour mixture and, using a wooden spoon, fold the ingredients together until no lumps remain. Stir in the mashed bananas.

3. Preheat the oven to 200°F.

4. In a griddle pan or nonstick skillet set over medium heat, add enough clarified butter to coat the bottom of the pan. When the butter is hot, spoon ¼-cup portions of batter onto the hot griddle. Cook until golden brown on one side, about 1½ minutes. Flip the fritters and cook until the second side is brown, about 2 minutes. Turn the heat down to medium-low if the fritters are cooking too quickly. Transfer the fritter to an ovenproof plate. Keep warm in the oven while you cook the rest of the fritters. Repeat the cooking process with the remaining batter, adding more clarified butter to the pan as necessary.

5. Serve warm with maple syrup and confectioners' sugar.

2 cups all-purpose flour

3 tablespoons packed light brown sugar

1½ teaspoons baking powder

1 teaspoon baking soda

1 teaspoon ground cinnamon

½ teaspoon freshly grated nutmeg

1 teaspoon salt

4 tablespoons Browned Butter (recipe follows)

2 large eggs

1½ cups buttermilk

3 overripe bananas, mashed

Clarified Butter (page 57) or canola oil, for the pan

Pure maple syrup, for serving

Confectioners' sugar, for serving

HOW TO BROWN BUTTER

There is absolutely nothing like browned butter. Made by cooking butter until it turns, well, brown, it has an amazing nutty flavor that brings a whole new dimension to your cooking. It shines brightest in baked goods, but try it out on other things too; it worked great in my Banana Fritters (opposite)!

Unsalted butter (however much you need for the recipe you want to make)

In a medium skillet set over medium heat, melt the butter. Cook until completely melted, swirling it in the pan occasionally. It'll foam and froth as it cooks, and then start to crackle and pop. Once the crackling stops, keep a close eye on the melted butter, continuing to swirl the pan often. The butter will start to smell nutty, and brown bits will form in the bottom of the pan. Cook until the bits are amber brown, another 2½ to 3 minutes. Immediately pour the butter into a small bowl to stop it from cooking and let cool for 20 minutes. Browned butter can be stored in an airtight container and refrigerated.

EARL GREY AND RICOTTA WAFFLES
WITH HONEY SWEET CREAM

SERVES 4

These tea-infused waffles are airy and fluffy, like little breakfast cakes topped with honey-sweetened whipped cream. Earl Grey tea has a distinct taste thanks to the essence of bergamot, and I think the flavor adds an extra-special touch to these waffles. I like using ricotta in the batter to get a lighter waffle, but sour cream will also do.

1. **FOR THE WAFFLES:** Preheat a waffle iron.

2. In a liquid measuring cup, microwave the milk until it is just bubbling, 45 seconds. Add the tea bags, cover, and let steep for 8 to 10 minutes. Squeeze any excess liquid from the tea bags and discard them.

3. In a medium bowl, whisk together the flour, baking powder, baking soda, salt, and sugar.

4. In a bowl or large measuring cup, whisk together the milky tea, butter, eggs, vanilla, and ricotta. Pour the tea mixture all at once into the flour mixture and stir to combine. Try not to overmix the batter; it's OK if a few lumps remain.

5. Dollop ¼-cup portions of batter onto the hot waffle iron. Cook until golden brown according to your waffle iron's instructions. Transfer to a wire cooling rack until ready to serve.

6. **FOR THE CREAM TOPPING:** In a medium bowl, combine the cream, honey, salt, and vanilla. Using an electric hand mixer, beat the cream 3 to 5 minutes, until soft peaks form.

7. Divide the waffles among four plates and dollop with the cream topping.

WAFFLES
¾ cup whole milk

2 Earl Grey tea bags

1½ cups all-purpose flour

2 teaspoons baking powder

½ teaspoon baking soda

½ teaspoon salt

3 tablespoons sugar

⅓ cup unsalted butter, melted

2 large eggs

1 teaspoon pure vanilla extract

½ cup part-skim milk ricotta cheese

CREAM TOPPING
1½ cups heavy whipping cream

3 tablespoons honey

Pinch of salt

Splash of pure vanilla extract

BREAKFAST BURRITOS

It was one of those Monday mornings when I decided I wanted pizza for breakfast. Unfortunately, the pizza restaurant down the street was closed, so I wandered a few blocks farther to my favorite breakfast spot, Elizabeth's (famous for their Praline Bacon, page 130). Their genius menu includes a French toast burrito, which combines a sweet flour tortilla and a salty, cheesy egg filling. My version of this breakfast hybrid is made with a crepe-like egg batter. The tortillas are dipped and fried in a shallow bath of hot oil, creating a lightly crisp but still pliable tortilla. This recipe is surprising and irresistible.

1. In a medium bowl, whisk together the milk, eggs, granulated sugar, and salt. Whisk in the flour and cinnamon until smooth. Let the batter rest for 20 minutes.

2. Meanwhile, in a medium skillet set over medium heat, add 1 tablespoon of the oil and cook the sausage, using the back of a spoon to break it up as it browns, about 6 minutes. Add the cayenne pepper and maple syrup and cook, stirring, about 4 more minutes, until crispy and caramelized. Remove the pan from the heat.

3. Heat the remaining the oil in a large skillet set over medium heat. Dip one tortilla in the egg batter, coating both sides. Drip any excess batter back into the bowl and gently place the tortilla in the hot oil. Fry about 1 minute per side, until golden brown on both sides. Transfer to a wire rack. Repeat with the remaining tortillas.

4. To assemble, spoon about a heaping 1/3 cup of cooked sausage into each fried tortilla. Sprinkle with cheese, top with scrambled eggs, gently fold in one side of the tortilla, and roll it up. Dust with confectioners' sugar and serve warm.

1/4 cup plus 2 tablespoons whole milk

2 large eggs

2 tablespoons granulated sugar

1/4 teaspoon salt

1/2 cup all-purpose flour

1/4 teaspoon ground cinnamon

3 tablespoons canola oil

3/4 pound mild Italian sausage, casings removed

1/4 teaspoon cayenne pepper

2 tablespoons pure maple syrup, plus more for serving

4 (10-inch) flour tortillas

3/4 cup grated sharp cheddar cheese

4 large eggs, scrambled (see page 55)

Confectioners' sugar, for serving

BUTTERED-PECAN FRENCH TOAST
WITH BOURBON MAPLE SYRUP

SERVES 4

I was never much of a fan of French toast until I discovered the wonders of brioche. It turns out that this dish, usually made with half-stale whole-wheat sandwich bread, is a very different thing when it's made with fresh, buttery, eggy brioche! I added the Southern-inspired buttered pecans and bourbon maple syrup, because this is the delicious world I live in.

1. **FOR THE BUTTERED PECANS:** Place a rack in the upper third of the oven and preheat to 350°F.

2. Place the pecan pieces on a rimmed baking sheet and toast for 10 to 14 minutes, until fragrant and golden brown. Remove from the oven and reduce the oven temperature to 200°F.

3. In a medium sauté pan set over medium heat, melt the butter. Stir in the sugar and salt. Add the pecans and cook, stirring, for 3 to 4 minutes, until the butter is lightly browned. Remove the pan from the heat.

4. **FOR THE FRENCH TOAST:** In a medium bowl, whisk together the eggs and milk.

5. In a small saucepan set over medium heat, warm the heavy cream for about 3 minutes, until just steaming and remove from the heat.

6. In a small bowl, combine the brown sugar, cinnamon, and salt. Add the sugar mixture to the cream and stir just until the sugar is dissolved. Add the cream mixture to the egg and milk mixture. Stir in the vanilla.

BUTTERED PECANS
I heaping cup pecan halves, coarsely chopped

3 tablespoons unsalted butter

I teaspoon sugar

½ teaspoon salt

FRENCH TOAST
5 large eggs

I cup whole milk

½ cup heavy cream

3 tablespoons lightly packed light brown sugar

½ teaspoon ground cinnamon

¼ teaspoon salt

2 teaspoons pure vanilla extract

8 thick slices brioche

4 tablespoons Clarified Butter (page 57), for the pan

BOURBON MAPLE SYRUP
I cup pure maple syrup

2 tablespoons bourbon

Dash of pure vanilla extract

Confectioners' sugar, for serving

(recipe continues)

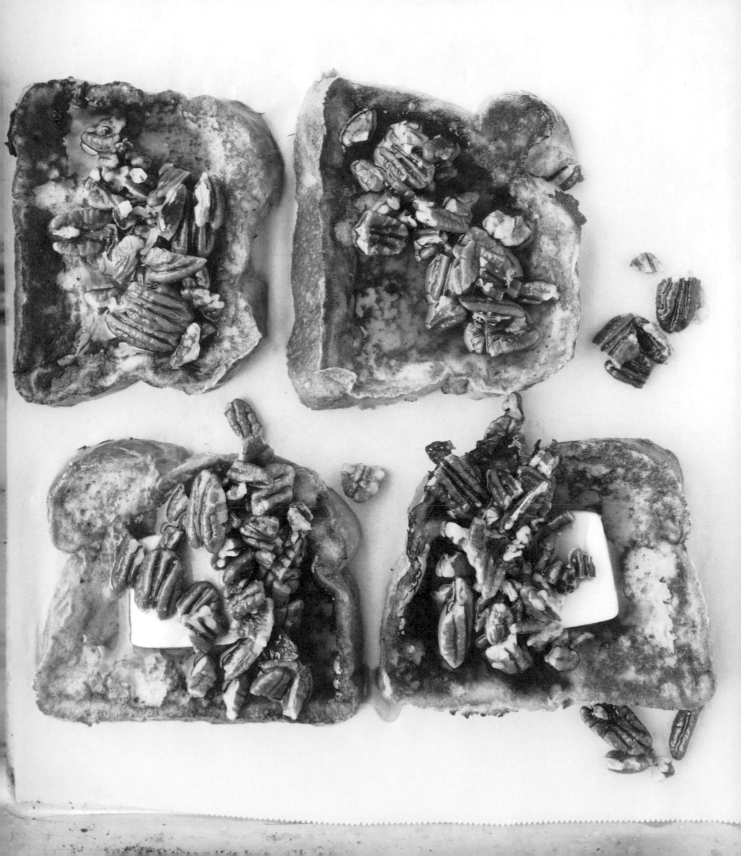

7. Working with one slice of bread at a time, put a slice into the egg mixture and let it soak for about 15 seconds on each side. Place on a rimmed baking sheet to rest while all the bread is dipped and the pan is heated.

8. In a medium nonstick skillet or griddle pan set over medium heat, melt the clarified butter. Place 2 or 3 bread slices into the pan and cook for about 2 minutes per side, until golden brown on each side. Add a bit more butter to the pan after you flip the bread, if needed. Transfer to a heatproof plate or rimmed baking sheet with a wire cooling rack set inside. Cover with a kitchen towel and keep warm in the oven while you cook the rest of the toast. Repeat the cooking process with the remaining bread.

9. **FOR THE BOURBON MAPLE SYRUP**: In a small saucepan set over low heat, gently stir together the maple syrup, bourbon, and vanilla until just warmed and well combined.

10. To serve, place 2 slices of French toast on each plate. Generously sprinkle with buttered pecans, drizzle with syrup, and dust with confectioners' sugar. Serve immediately.

BLUEBERRY SOUR CREAM WAFFLES
WITH MAPLE GLAZE

SERVES 4

These waffles have all the qualities of a fresh, heavily fruited blueberry muffin, combined with a maple syrup glaze inspired by donuts. I think these are lovely served room temperature piled onto a platter at a bountiful brunch table that also includes Grapefruit Rosemary Mimosas (page 23) and Shakshuka with Feta and Parsley (page 82).

1. **FOR THE WAFFLES:** Preheat a waffle iron.

2. In a large bowl, whisk together the flour, baking powder, baking soda, salt, and sugar.

3. In a medium bowl, whisk together the butter, eggs, vanilla extract, sour cream, and milk until smooth. Pour the mixture all at once into the flour mixture and stir until just incorporated. Stir in the blueberries. Try not to overmix the batter; if a few lumps remain, that's OK.

4. Dollop ¼-cup portions of batter onto the hot waffle iron. Cook until golden brown according to your waffle iron's instructions. Transfer to a wire cooling rack until ready to serve.

5. **FOR THE GLAZE:** In a small bowl, whisk together the confectioners' sugar, butter, maple syrup, and 1 tablespoon of the milk. Stir until smooth and just pourable, adding the remaining 1 tablespoon milk if needed.

6. Before serving, dip the top of each waffle into the maple glaze, set them on plates, and top with fresh blueberries.

WAFFLES

1½ cups all-purpose flour

2 teaspoons baking powder

½ teaspoon baking soda

½ teaspoon salt

3 tablespoons granulated sugar

⅓ cup unsalted butter, melted

2 large eggs

2 teaspoons pure vanilla extract

1 cup sour cream

¼ cup whole milk

1 heaping cup fresh blueberries, plus more for serving

GLAZE

2 cups confectioners' sugar

2 tablespoons unsalted butter, melted

3 tablespoons pure maple syrup

1 to 2 tablespoons whole milk

CORNBREAD WAFFLES

SERVES 4

Every serious bruncher (and that's definitely you) has a waffle iron. It doesn't matter if you have to dig it out from the way-back of a cabinet, or tug it fresh out of the box from the wedding present pile. You brunch, therefore you waffle.

These cornbread waffles are versatile. They're delicious served with sliced bananas and maple syrup, and equally delightful topped with chicken salad, or sandwiched around fried chicken. For future breakfasts, these waffles also freeze well and toast up warm and fresh. They're delicious with crisp fried eggs (see page 58) and a big side of Praline Bacon (page 130).

¾ cup coarse yellow cornmeal

¾ cup all-purpose flour

I teaspoon baking powder

I teaspoon baking soda

Pinch of freshly grated nutmeg

½ teaspoon salt

2 tablespoons honey

I tablespoon molasses (optional)

I cup buttermilk

4 tablespoons Browned Butter (page 97)

I large egg

1. Preheat a waffle iron.

2. In a medium bowl, whisk together the cornmeal, flour, baking powder, baking soda, nutmeg, and salt.

3. In a separate bowl, whisk together the honey, molasses (if using), buttermilk, browned butter, and egg. Pour the mixture all at once into the cornmeal mixture and stir well. Let sit for 10 minutes.

4. Dollop ¼-cup portions of batter onto the hot waffle iron. Cook until golden brown according to your waffle iron's instructions. Transfer to a wire cooling rack until ready to serve.

GREEN PEA FRITTERS

SERVES 6

These are not maple syrup–doused pancakes. They're the savory sort and super versatile. You can substitute half of the peas for sweet corn, if you like, and try serving with poached or fried eggs for a simple breakfast. I love to top the warm fritters with smoked salmon, a dollop of sour cream, and fresh herbs, too.

1. Bring a medium pot of salted water to a boil. Add the peas and cook for 4 minutes, until warmed through. Drain and transfer to the bowl of a food processor fitted with the regular chopping blade. Add the garlic, parsley, mint, chives, lemon zest, 1 teaspoon salt, and pepper. Pulse for 30 seconds to just combine.

2. In a small bowl, whisk together the sour cream, eggs, and lemon juice. Add the sour cream mixture to the food processor and pulse for about 2 minutes, until the mixture is well combined and the peas are broken down. Transfer to a medium bowl, stir in the flour, and let rest for 10 minutes.

3. On a griddle or in a nonstick skillet set over medium heat, melt 1 tablespoon clarified butter. Scoop ¼-cup portions of the batter onto the griddle and flatten slightly. Cook for about 2 minutes, until golden brown. Flip and cook for 2 more minutes, until golden on the second side. Transfer to a wire rack. Repeat with the remaining batter, adding more clarified butter to the pan as necessary. Serve warm.

I teaspoon salt, plus more for the water

I pound frozen green peas, thawed

I garlic clove, minced

¼ cup coarsely chopped fresh parsley

3 tablespoons coarsely chopped fresh mint

3 tablespoons chopped fresh chives

I teaspoon finely grated lemon zest

½ teaspoon freshly cracked black pepper

½ cup sour cream

2 large eggs, lightly beaten

2 tablespoons fresh lemon juice

½ cup all-purpose flour

3 tablespoons Clarified Butter (page 57), for the pan

EGG IN A HOLE

SERVES 4

This classic kids' breakfast is perfectly delicious with simple sliced sandwich bread, but the key to making it brunchworthy is to buy a fresh loaf of really great bread and the freshest eggs you can find. The fewer the ingredients in a recipe, the more spectacular they should be. I love a crusty sourdough loaf. Slice it nice and thick, and for extra deliciousness, serve with Spinach and Almond Pesto (page 142).

4 (1- to 1½-inch-thick) slices of fresh bread

3 tablespoons Clarified Butter (page 57)

4 large eggs

Salt

Freshly cracked black pepper

1. Using a 2-inch round biscuit cutter (or the top of a small glass), cut a hole in the center of the bread slices and remove the bread round.

2. On a griddle or in a nonstick skillet set over medium heat, melt half of the clarified butter. Put the bread on the griddle and toast until golden brown, about 2 minutes. Flip the bread and add the remaining butter, tilting the pan to spread the butter across the pan. Crack an egg into the center of each hole in the bread. Season each egg with salt and pepper, reduce the heat to low, and cover with foil. Cook for 2 to 3 minutes, until the bread is golden and the egg whites are set on the bottom. Serve warm.

MASHED POTATO SKILLET SCONES

MAKES 10 TO 12 SCONES

These stovetop-cooked scones are buttery-crisp on the outside and creamy mashed potatoes on the inside. It's like the most comforting dish at the dinner table went incognito at brunch. I've found that these scones are best made in a nonstick skillet or on a griddle pan coated well in fat to keep them from sticking. Serve warm with loads of sour cream and chives, fried eggs (see page 58), and lots of coffee.

2 large russet potatoes, peeled and cut into large chunks

6 tablespoons unsalted butter, at room temperature

2 tablespoons sour cream, plus more for serving

1 tablespoon fresh chopped chives, plus more for serving

1 scant teaspoon salt, plus more as needed

¾ teaspoon freshly cracked black pepper, plus more as needed

¾ cup all-purpose flour, plus more for rolling

¾ teaspoon baking powder

Clarified Butter (page 57), for the pan

1. Place the potato chunks in a large saucepan and cover with cool water. Set the pan over medium-high heat and bring to a boil. Boil until tender, 10 to 12 minutes. Drain and let cool for 5 minutes. Press the cooked potatoes through a ricer or the holes of a colander and back into the saucepan. Add the butter, the sour cream, chives, salt, and pepper and stir well.

2. In a small bowl, whisk together the flour, baking powder, and season with a bit more salt and pepper. Add the flour mixture to the potato mixture and use a wooden spoon to stir until just combined. The mixture may still be very warm at this point. Let rest until cool enough to handle.

3. Using a lightly floured rolling pin, roll the dough out on a lightly floured work surface to ¾-inch thick. Use a 2½-inch round biscuit cutter (or the top of a small glass) to cut rounds and place them on a rimmed baking sheet. Flour the biscuit cutter as needed so the scones don't stick. Reroll the scraps to create as many rounds as possible. Refrigerate for 30 minutes.

4. On a griddle or in a medium skillet set over medium heat, heat about 1 tablespoon of clarified butter until very hot. Place up to four scones in the skillet at a time. Cook for about 4 minutes per side, until deliciously crisp and golden brown on both sides. Transfer to paper towels to drain. Repeat with the remaining dough, adding more fat to the pan as necessary. Enjoy warm.

SIDES

When I gather friends around the breakfast table, their morning meal personalities shine through via the side dishes. For some friends, potatoes reign supreme. They must be crisp and golden, extra buttery, and properly salted. For others, it's all about the meat, and they make no qualms about hoarding slices of Praline Bacon (page 130) on their plate (little do they know I have a secret stash tucked away in the kitchen). For a few folks, it's all about vegetables, and they want nothing more than crispy Brussels sprouts to accompany their eggs. Whatever the preference or hoarding tendencies, sides add delicious variety and a ton of personality to the table.

Brunch is all about that extra something special—the extra time spent, the extra freshly cracked black peppercorn, the extra cheese in the grits. It's care and attention that take a meal from breakfast to something shared and memorable. Nestle these recipes next to poached eggs and stacks of waffles, and share them with gusto. They're also meant to be simple and arm you with know-how in the kitchen, with recipes like skillet hash made from refrigerator leftovers and tricks to make the crispiest hash browns to forever keep in your repertoire. As long as the sides are plentiful, with enough bacon to offset the hoarders, your brunch will be a special affair.

VERY CRISPY HASH BROWNS

We've all suffered through enough dreadfully soggy, overly greasy, crime-against-potatoes hash browns. No more. We've got to rage against the soggy potato. I'm going to teach you some tricks for thoroughly crisp, golden-brown, buttery hash browns. Perfect potatoes don't happen by accident.

3 large or 4 medium russet potatoes, peeled

¾ to 1 teaspoon coarse sea salt

½ teaspoon freshly cracked black pepper

¼ teaspoon smoked paprika

6 tablespoons Clarified Butter (page 57)

Hot sauce, for serving

Sour cream, for serving

1. Fill a large bowl halfway full with cool water.

2. Using the coarse side of a box grater, grate the potatoes. As the grated potato piles up, scoop the potato shreds into the bowl of water. Using your hand, swirl the potatoes around in the water for about 1 minute. The water will become cloudy as some of the starch is released from the potatoes.

3. Drain the potatoes and rinse under cool water for 2 minutes, stirring and moving the potatoes around with your hand as they're rinsing. Scoop half of the potatoes into a clean kitchen towel. Gather the edges of the towel and twist to tighten, squeezing out the water from the potatoes. Squeeze well and then squeeze again. Transfer the potatoes to a medium bowl. Repeat with the remaining grated potatoes.

4. To the potatoes, add the salt, pepper, and paprika. Using your hands, toss well.

5. In a large nonstick skillet set over medium heat, melt 2 tablespoons of the clarified butter. Add half of the seasoned potatoes to the pan, press into a single thin layer, increase the heat to medium-high, and cook undisturbed for 2 minutes. Check that the potatoes are golden brown, then break into four rough pieces and flip the pieces over.

(recipe continues)

6. Add 1 more tablespoon of clarified butter as the other side cooks. Cook for 2 minutes, until golden brown. Reduce the heat to medium and occasionally toss and stir the potatoes until they are cooked through, 8 to 10 minutes total. Transfer to a plate.

7. Add 2 more tablespoons of clarified butter and cook the remaining potatoes, adding the remaining 1 tablespoon of butter as necessary. Serve warm with hot sauce and sour cream.

TIPS FOR GREAT HASH BROWNS

• Pick firm, starchy potatoes for crisp, golden hash browns. Peeled russet potatoes are best.

• Putting the grated potatoes in cool water keeps them from browning, which happens when they are exposed to air. It will also help to remove some of the starch (you'll see the water get cloudy). Once the potatoes are soaked, rinse them.

• Squeezing the potatoes dry is very important. Opt for a clean linen (not terry cloth) towel, and squeeze the shredded potatoes in two batches. Squeeze really hard!

• Since the potatoes cook at such a high heat, it's important to use a fat that won't burn. The milk solids in butter have a tendency to brown (which is delicious) and quickly burn (which is not as delicious). Clarified butter is the perfect solution (see page 57). Also, a large nonstick skillet is necessary.

• Once the potatoes are in the pan, it's just a matter of time and patience. Let them cook undisturbed initially, and don't rush the process.

ROASTED HOME FRIES

SERVES 4 TO 6

What's the difference between roasted potatoes at dinner and roasted potatoes at breakfast? I've determined that it's not necessarily the ingredients; it's the size of the dice. Home fries, the clever name for homemade breakfast potatoes, are diced smaller—to about ½ inch—than their dinner counterparts. In addition to onions and peppers, I like to toss in carrots for an extra touch of sweetness.

1. Place a rack in the upper third of the oven and preheat to 375°F. Line a rimmed baking sheet with foil.

2. Scrub the potatoes and cut them into uniform ½-inch pieces. Put the potatoes into a medium bowl and add the onions, bell pepper, and carrots. Drizzle with olive oil, season generously with salt and pepper, and toss well. Transfer to the prepared baking sheet and spread into a single layer. Dot or drizzle the clarified butter over the vegetables.

3. Roast for 15 minutes. Stir the vegetables and roast 15 to 20 more minutes, until cooked through and golden brown. Let cool slightly before transferring to a platter and serving.

8 small or medium red new potatoes

1 small yellow onion, finely chopped

1 green bell pepper, seeded, and finely chopped

2 carrots, chopped

2 tablespoons olive oil

Sea salt

Freshly cracked black pepper

2 tablespoons Clarified Butter (page 57)

SMASHED PAN-FRIED PLANTAINS

SERVES 4 TO 6

Plantains are large, firm, starchy bananas. Because they're so firm and full of starch, they hold up very well to pan-frying for a dish called *tostones*. Sweet but not overly so, they bring an intriguing element to savory egg dishes. I especially love these alongside Huevos Rancheros (page 77), though they're delicious on their own with a tall michelada (page 13).

¼ cup canola oil

3 ripe plantains (they'll be yellow and speckled), peeled and sliced just under ½ inch thick

Salt and freshly cracked black pepper

Smoked paprika, for serving

In a medium nonstick skillet set over medium heat, heat the oil. Add the plantain slices to cover the bottom of the skillet with enough room to flip. Fry for about 2 minutes per side, until golden brown on both sides. Transfer to a paper towel–lined plate and use the bottom of a pint glass to gently smash each fried plantain. Sprinkle with salt, pepper, and paprika. Repeat with the remaining plantains. Serve warm.

GOETTA SLICES

MAKES 1 LOAF

Let's take a little trip to Cincinnati, Ohio, via breakfast sausage. Goetta (pronounced get-uh)—a mixture of ground meat and steel-cut oats that is pressed together, chilled, sliced, and fried on a griddle—is popular in Cincinnati, thanks to the city's German population. German peasants created this staple, using oats to extend the meat. Goetta is closely related to scrapple, which uses cornmeal instead of oats. My goetta recipe is fairly straightforward, and is delicious served with either sweet or savory condiments—ketchup and maple syrup being my absolute favorites. Serve with Fluffy Scrambled Eggs (page 55).

4 tablespoons canola oil

I pound boneless chuck, cut into I-inch pieces

I pound pork shoulder, cut into I-inch pieces

½ cup yellow onion, chopped

I cup steel-cut oats

I garlic clove

2 teaspoons fresh thyme leaves

2 tablespoons Worcestershire sauce

Salt and freshly cracked black pepper

Clarified Butter (page 57), for the pan

1. In a medium saucepan set over medium heat, heat 2 tablespoons oil. Add the chuck and cook for 5 to 7 minutes, until browned on all sides. The meat won't be cooked through; that's okay. Transfer to a plate. Heat the remaining 2 tablespoons oil. Add the pork shoulder and cook for 5 to 7 minutes, until browned on all sides. Transfer to the plate with the beef.

2. Add the onions to the pan and cook, stirring, for 4 to 6 minutes, until soft and lightly browned. Transfer to a small bowl.

3. Return the beef and pork to the pan and add 3 to 4 cups of water—enough to mostly, but not completely, cover the meat. Reduce the heat to low. Cover the pan and cook for 1½ to 2 hours, until the meat is tender and cooked through.

4. While the meat is cooking, bring 3½ cups of water to a boil in a medium saucepan. Add the oats, reduce the heat to low, cover, and simmer for 30 minutes, until the water has absorbed.

(recipe continues)

5. Transfer the cooked meat to the bowl of a food processor fitted with the regular chopping blade. Reserve about 1 cup of the simmering liquid. Let the meat cool for 15 minutes.

6. To the food processor, add the oats, cooked onions, garlic, thyme, Worcestershire sauce, ½ cup of reserved liquid, salt, and pepper. Process until the mixture is a thick, slightly coarse paste, adding a bit more of the simmering liquid if necessary.

7. Line a 9 × 5-inch loaf pan with plastic wrap, leaving about 4 inches to hang over the sides. Press the meat mixture into the pan and cover with the extra plastic wrap. Refrigerate overnight.

8. To serve, heat about 3 tablespoons of clarified butter in a heavy-bottomed skillet set over medium-high heat. Unwrap the goetta and pull it from the pan. Cut it into ¾-inch-thick slices. Add the slices to the pan, working in batches if necessary, and cook for about 2 minutes per side, until golden brown on each side. Serve warm.

BEER-BRAISED
KIELBASA, POTATOES, AND ONIONS

SERVES 4 TO 6

Meat and potatoes together at last! Big bite-size pieces of sausage are braised with new potatoes and onions for a hearty and saucy side dish. I love these potatoes served with poached eggs and toast. When choosing a beer, I went with a light and friendly beer. The more strongly flavored pale ales can add unwanted bitterness to the dish. This is a hearty dish on its own, made all the more satisfying with a side of poached eggs (see page 60). (See photograph, page 114.)

3 tablespoons canola oil

2 pounds cooked kielbasa (pork or turkey), cut into 2-inch chunks

1 large yellow onion, sliced

1 pound small new potatoes, cut into quarters

Sea salt

Freshly cracked black pepper

1 cup chicken stock

1 cup light beer

2 sprigs fresh thyme

2 tablespoons unsalted butter

2 tablespoons all-purpose flour

¼ cup coarsely chopped fresh parsley, for garnish

2 tablespoons chopped fresh chives, for garnish

1. In a large skillet, heat 2 tablespoons oil over medium heat. Add the kielbasa and cook, stirring occasionally, for 8 to 10 minutes, until browned on all sides. Transfer to a plate.

2. Add the onions to the pan and cook, stirring, for 4 to 6 minutes, until translucent and just beginning to brown. Add the remaining 1 tablespoon of oil to the pan and add the potatoes. Cook, stirring occasionally, until the potatoes begin to soften, 6 to 8 minutes. Season with salt and pepper. Add the stock and beer, scraping up any browned bits stuck to the bottom of the pan. Add the thyme. Scatter the kielbasa on top of the potatoes and add any juices that collected in the plate. Cover the pan, reduce the heat to low, and simmer undisturbed for 20 to 25 minutes, until the potatoes are soft and cooked through.

3. Using a slotted spoon, transfer the sausage, potatoes, and onions to a platter.

4. In a small skillet set over medium heat, melt the butter. Whisk in the flour and cook, whisking constantly, for 1 minute. Slowly stream in 1 to 1½ cups of the warm cooking broth and cook, whisking, until it thickens into a pourable gravy. Pour the gravy over the potatoes and sausage. Sprinkle with parsley and chives, and serve warm.

SAUTÉED SHREDDED
BRUSSELS SPROUTS

SERVES 2

It's easy to think you don't like Brussels sprouts—and if that's the case for you, it's likely you haven't had them cooked correctly. I think all of us have been traumatized by our grandmother's rendition of mushy boiled Brussels sprouts. Not to worry, though, they are now illegal in forty-seven states.

These sprouts are transformed into ribbons, sautéed at a high heat so they soften and crisp, creating a hearty and satisfying side. When served with poached eggs and crisp bacon, this dish is a complete and incredibly delicious meal! This recipe is easily doubled or tripled if you're making sprouts for many.

½ pound Brussels sprouts

2 tablespoons olive oil

I small shallot, finely chopped

I garlic clove, minced

Salt

Freshly cracked black pepper

Juice of ½ lemon

Shaved Parmesan, for serving

¼ teaspoon smoked paprika, for serving

1. Thinly slice the sprouts horizontally into thirds, creating thick ribbons.

2. In a medium skillet, heat the oil over medium. Add the shallot and cook, stirring, for about 4 minutes, until translucent and just browned. Add the garlic and cook, stirring, 1 minute more. Add the sprout ribbons and increase the heat to medium-high. Cook, stirring, for about 6 minutes, until the sprouts have softened and begun to brown. Season with salt and pepper. Remove the pan from the heat and stir in the lemon juice.

3. Divide among serving bowls, top with cheese and paprika, and serve warm.

PRALINE BACON

MAKES 12 SLICES

This bacon has a place at every single one of my brunch tables. It's the answer to every question, especially if it's "What's for breakfast and can it please be the most delicious thing ever?" Yes. Thick-cut bacon that's been covered in brown sugar and baked—we're calling it "praline" because the concept was invented at Elizabeth's in the Bywater. Our hearts, and bacon, are in New Orleans.

I pound thick-sliced bacon (12 slices)

2 tablespoons finely chopped pecans

¼ cup packed light brown sugar

¼ teaspoon freshly cracked black pepper

1. Place a rack in the upper third of the oven and preheat to 400°F.

2. Line a rimmed baking sheet with foil and lay the bacon slices in a single layer. Bake for 10 minutes.

3. In a small bowl, toss together the pecans, sugar, and pepper. Remove the bacon from the oven and sprinkle with the sugar mixture.

4. Bake for 10 to 12 more minutes, until browned and bubbling.

HEARTS OF PALM FRIES

SERVES 4

Hearts of palm are, as their name suggests, the center of palm stalks. They're most often found canned, alongside jars of pickles or cans of artichoke hearts. The tender, salty spears, when cut into sticks and fried, make intriguing fries. Simply sprinkled with lemon juice and spicy pickled japaleño slices, they're excellent paired with the Breakfast Burger (page 156).

Canola oil, for frying

1½ cups bread crumbs

1½ cups panko bread crumbs, crushed

1 teaspoon Old Bay seasoning

Scant 1 teaspoon freshly cracked black pepper

1 cup all-purpose flour

2 large eggs

½ cup buttermilk

1 teaspoon hot sauce

2 (28-ounce) cans hearts of palm, cut into quarters

Lemon wedges, for serving

Sliced pickled jalapeños, for serving

Sea salt, for serving

1. In a medium saucepan fitted with a deep-fry thermometer, heat about 2½ inches of oil to 350°F over medium. Line a sheet pan with paper towels and set aside.

2. While the oil is heating, in a medium bowl, combine both types of bread crumbs, ½ teaspoon of Old Bay seasoning, and ½ teaspoon pepper.

3. In a separate bowl, combine the flour, the remaining ½ teaspoon Old Bay, and the remaining ½ teaspoon pepper.

4. In yet another bowl, beat the eggs, buttermilk, and hot sauce.

5. Coat each heart of palm spear in the flour mixture. Then lightly coat in the buttermilk mixture, and finally coat in the bread crumb mixture.

6. Working in batches of four to six spears at a time, fry for 2 to 3 minutes, until golden brown on all sides. Using a slotted spoon, transfer to the paper towel–lined sheet pan to blot the oil. Bring the frying oil back up to 350°F before each batch.

7. Serve immediately with lemon wedges, pickled jalapeños, and coarse sea salt.

SPICY BROWN SUGAR
SAUSAGE PATTIES

SERVES 4 TO 6

Making your own sausage patties means that you get to control exactly how sweet, spicy, and flavorful you want them to be. I love adding dry mustard and brown sugar, which balance beautifully with the fennel and bay leaf. I've used ground pork, though ground turkey would also be delicious (be sure to choose the higher-fat thigh meat). These patties freeze well for your future brunch-self.

1. In a spice grinder, or with a mortar and pestle, combine the bay leaf, red pepper flakes, mustard, nutmeg, fennel, and cloves. Pulse until you have a fine powder.

2. In a medium bowl, combine the ground spice mixture with the pork, chives, brown sugar, salt, and pepper. Using your hands or a spoon, thoroughly combine the ingredients.

3. In a heavy-bottomed skillet set over medium heat, heat 2 tablespoons of oil. Divide the meat mixture into twelve portions and shape into 1-inch-thick patties. Working in batches, cook the sausage patties 5 to 6 minutes per side, until browned on both sides, adding more oil as necessary between batches. Transfer to paper towels to drain, and serve warm.

4. To freeze, individually wrap the cooked patties in plastic wrap and store for up to 2 months in the freezer. To reheat, gently warm in a greased skillet.

I dried bay leaf

I teaspoon crushed red pepper flakes

I teaspoon dry mustard

¾ teaspoon freshly grated nutmeg

Scant I teaspoon fennel seeds, toasted and lightly crushed

Pinch of ground cloves

I pound ground pork

3 tablespoons chopped fresh chives

I tablespoon packed brown sugar

2 teaspoons kosher salt

2 teaspoons freshly cracked black pepper

4 tablespoons canola oil, for frying

ROASTED CHERRY TOMATOES
ON THE VINE

SERVES 4

With some quality time in the oven, fresh cherry tomatoes transform from vegetable to candy as their flavor and sweetness intensify to irresistible proportions. I love these served alongside Fluffy Scrambled Eggs (page 55) with Very Crispy Hash Browns (page 117). Tomatoes on the vine are easiest to find during the warmer summer months. If you can't find those, regular cherry tomatoes will be just as delicious. If you use tomatoes without the vine, slice some of them in half before baking.

I pound cherry tomatoes on the vine

3 tablespoons olive oil

1½ teaspoons coarse sea salt

I teaspoon freshly cracked black pepper

I teaspoon fresh thyme leaves

1. Place a rack in the center of the oven and preheat to 375°F. Line a rimmed baking sheet with parchment paper.

2. Place the tomatoes onto the prepared baking sheet. Drizzle with the olive oil, ½ teaspoon of salt, and pepper.

3. In a small bowl, rub together the remaining 1 teaspoon salt with the thyme.

4. Roast the tomatoes until bursting and bubbling, 25 to 30 minutes. Remove from the oven. Sprinkle with thyme salt and let cool slightly before serving.

SAUSAGE GRAVY

SERVES 6

Push aside the fruit parfait and that green juice smoothie. Some morning meals require a more stick-to-your-ribs approach. This creamy, hearty sausage gravy is a most decadent topping for Dad's Buttermilk Biscuits (page 218) and a side of hard fried eggs (page 58). I recommend accompanying said gravy and biscuits with Grapefruit Rosemary Mimosas (page 23) and a long afternoon nap.

1. In a large skillet set over medium heat, cook the sausage, using a wooden spoon to break up the meat, for 8 to 10 minutes, until cooked through. Add the sage, thyme, and garlic powder and cook for 1 minute more. Sprinkle the flour over the sizzling sausage and stir until the flour is absorbed, about 2 minutes. Reduce the heat to low and, while whisking constantly, slowly pour in 3 cups of milk. Cook, whisking constantly, until thick, about 4 minutes. Cook it a little longer if you like a thick gravy, or add the remaining ½ cup of milk, if needed, to thin it out.

2. Remove the pan from the heat. Season to taste with salt and pepper. Serve warm. The gravy will keep for 2 days in an airtight container in the refrigerator. Reheat it in a saucepan with a splash more milk.

I pound Italian sausage (spicy or mild)

¼ teaspoon ground sage

¼ teaspoon dried thyme

½ teaspoon garlic powder

⅓ cup all-purpose flour

3 to 3½ cups whole milk, at room temperature

Sea salt

Freshly cracked black pepper

BUTTERED GRITS AND TOPPINGS

SERVES 4

Bring a pot of buttery grits to the table, and I swear, you can hear a collective sigh of both excitement and relief. Yesssss! Breakfast is going to be good! A big bowl of grits with a variety of toppings is an easy dish to serve a crowd. Guests can choose their own adventure. These grits are extra creamy and are allowed to sit and absorb the milk rather than boil away. You can make your brunch life rosy by making the grits and toppings ahead of time and warming just before serving—just be sure to add a dash more milk or cream to the grits so they're spoonable and soft.

1. **FOR THE GRITS:** Combine the water, milk, cream, butter, salt, and pepper in a medium saucepan with a tight-fitting lid. Set the pan over medium heat and bring to a simmer. Stir in the grits and bring to a simmer again. Cook, without stirring, for 1 to 2 minutes until the grits float to the surface. Cover, remove the pan from the heat, and let sit at least 10 minutes, until all of the moisture has been absorbed. The grits will be creamy. Whisk until smooth. Season with salt and pepper to taste. Whisk in additional milk as needed to reach the desired consistency.

2. **FOR THE SHRIMP:** In a medium skillet set over medium heat, melt the butter. Add the shrimp and cook for about 5 minutes, until pink throughout. Toss with salt, pepper, and lemon zest, and sprinkle with lemon juice. Garnish with paprika and parsley.

3. **FOR THE CHORIZO:** Heat the oil in a medium skillet set over medium heat. Add the chorizo and cook for about 6 minutes, using the back of a spoon to break the meat into small pieces as it browns. Drain most of the fat from the skillet. Add the corn and cook, stirring, for 4 minutes, until warmed through. Just before serving, sprinkle with the pepper, scallions, and cheese.

GRITS

1½ cups water

¾ cup whole milk, plus more as needed

¼ cup heavy cream

3 tablespoons unsalted butter

½ teaspoon kosher salt, plus more as needed

¼ teaspoon freshly cracked black pepper, plus more as needed

¾ cup yellow or white corn grits (not instant)

SHRIMP

3 tablespoons unsalted butter

12 shrimp, peeled and deveined, tails attached

Salt and freshly cracked black pepper

½ teaspoon grated fresh lemon zest

3 tablespoons fresh lemon juice

Smoked paprika, for garnish

Chopped fresh parsley, for garnish

CHORIZO

2 tablespoons canola oil

1 pound chorizo, casings removed

2 cups frozen corn, thawed and drained

½ teaspoon freshly cracked black pepper

½ cup thinly sliced scallions (both white and green parts)

1½ cups grated sharp cheddar cheese

4. **FOR THE ONIONS AND MUSHROOMS:** In a large skillet set over medium heat, add 3 tablespoons of the butter and 1 tablespoon of the olive oil, and stir until the butter is melted. Add the onions and stir to coat in the fat. Let cook, undisturbed, for about 4 minutes. Add the thyme and sugar, and season with salt and pepper. Cover and let cook, stirring occasionally, for about 6 minutes, until the onions resemble jam. Remove the lid to stir the onions every so often, and lower the heat if the onions are browning too quickly.

5. Transfer to a bowl, and add the remaining butter and oil to the pan. Add the mushrooms and stir to coat in the fat. Cook undisturbed for 4 minutes to let the mushrooms soften and release some water. They'll begin to brown and caramelize after about 6 minutes. Lower the heat if they begin to burn. Continue to cook for about 3 more minutes, until the mushrooms are broken down and well browned. Return the onions to the pan and stir well. Add the broth to the pan, scraping any bits from the bottom of the pan. Just before serving, sprinkle with the cheese and parsley.

6. To serve, ladle the grits into four small bowls, and then let each person pile on their own toppings and combinations.

ONIONS AND MUSHROOMS

6 tablespoons unsalted butter

2 tablespoons olive oil

2 medium yellow onions, sliced (about 3 cups)

2 teaspoons coarsely chopped fresh thyme leaves

Pinch of sugar

Salt and freshly cracked black pepper

1 pound cremini mushrooms, sliced

¼ cup beef, vegetable, or chicken broth

1 cup grated Gruyère cheese

¼ cup coarsely chopped fresh parsley

SPINACH AND ALMOND PESTO

MAKES ABOUT 1 CUP

Pesto is a super versatile brunch staple. Throw it on top of everything from scrambled eggs to a perfectly cooked steak, or stir it into Roasted Home Fries (page 120). Instead of basil, I like to make it with spinach, because it's easy to find year-round and makes for a beautiful, bright green pesto. If you like, try substituting roasted salted cashews for the almonds. Keep the pesto jarred in the fridge and you'll be surprised all the things you dollop it on!

Place the spinach, garlic, almonds, lemon juice, and cheese in the bowl of a food processor fitted with the regular chopping blade. Pulse until coarsely chopped. With the machine running, slowly drizzle in the olive oil and continue processing about 1 minute, until the mixture is well chopped and emulsified. The pesto will keep for up to 1 week in an airtight jar or container in the refrigerator.

2 packed and heaping cups spinach leaves

1 garlic clove

¼ cup coarsely chopped roasted salted almonds

2 tablespoons fresh lemon juice

⅓ cup grated Parmesan cheese

⅓ cup olive oil

VANILLA ROSEMARY YOGURT

SERVES 4

Because brunch is where we add a little flair, a drizzle of honey, and a hint of herbaceousness, I bring you a simple and sweet vanilla yogurt. While the yogurt is store-bought, all the glory is in the home-made herb-steeped honey. Serve with fresh berries and toasted almonds or with the Peaches and Cream with Honeyed Cornflakes (page 150).

⅓ cup honey, or more if desired
1 sprig fresh rosemary
1 vanilla bean
32 ounces plain yogurt

1. In a small saucepan set over low heat, combine the honey and rosemary. Split the vanilla pod and scrape the seeds into the pan. Whisk until the honey is warmed through and the rosemary is fragrant, but don't let the mixture simmer, about 4 minutes. Remove the pan from the heat and let cool for 5 minutes. Remove the rosemary sprig and scrape off the honey onto the yogurt before discarding the sprig.

2. Stir the honey into the yogurt and refrigerate, covered, until ready to serve.

BROILED GRAPEFRUIT

SERVES 4

Cooking is my love language. Making and sharing a meal with someone is how I show deep care. Now, segmenting a grapefruit for someone? That's a different level. Delicately slicing around each grapefruit segment—that means it's true love. Adding brown sugar and broiling until crunchy and sweet seals the deal.

2 large pink grapefruits, sliced in half

4 tablespoons packed light brown sugar

Pinch of ground cinnamon (optional)

Pinch of freshly grated nutmeg (optional)

1. Place a rack in the upper third of the oven and preheat the oven broiler. Line a rimmed baking sheet with foil and set aside.

2. Using a serrated knife, cut in between and around the grapefruit segments, which will make it easy to remove the grapefruit pieces from the grapefruit half. Sprinkle each grapefruit half with 1 tablespoon brown sugar. Add a pinch of cinnamon and nutmeg to each, if you'd like. Arrange the grapefruit halves on the prepared baking sheet.

3. Broil for about 3 minutes, until the tops are bubbling and golden brown and the sugar has begun to crystallize.

4. Using tongs, transfer the halves to small bowls. Serve warm.

COMPOUND BUTTERS

Let's make butter better! How? Loads of ways! With crumbled bacon, a splash of tequila, a handful of fresh herbs, some vanilla beans, or a heap of raisins. These gussied-up butters are perfect for spreading on Dad's Buttermilk Biscuits (page 218), and that's just the beginning. Go on, get fancy!

To make compound butter, start with 1 cup (2 sticks) good-quality unsalted butter, softened to a very pliable room temperature. There's no need for a mixer if your butter is soft enough. Put the softened butter in a medium bowl. Add a good pinch of sea salt. Stir in any of the following combinations. Spoon into a small ramekin, or place on a piece of plastic wrap and roll into a log, and refrigerate for at least 2 hours to allow the butter to firm up and the flavors to meld. The butters will keep in the refrigerator for up to 5 days.

TEQUILA-JALAPEÑO-LIME BUTTER. Remove and discard the seeds from 1 large or 2 small jalapeño peppers. Place in a small food processor with 2 tablespoons tequila and 1½ teaspoons fresh lime zest. Blend until finely ground. Stir the mixture into the softened butter.

BACON AND BLUE CHEESE BUTTER. Stir ⅓ cup crumbled cooked bacon, ½ cup crumbled blue cheese, and 2 tablespoons coarsely chopped parsley into the softened butter.

PARSLEY-LEMON-CHILI BUTTER. Stir 3 tablespoons chopped parsley, 1½ teaspoons grated fresh lemon zest, and 1 teaspoon crushed red pepper flakes into the softened butter.

WHOLE-GRAIN HONEY MUSTARD BUTTER. Stir 3 tablespoons whole-grain mustard and 2 tablespoons honey into the softened butter.

VANILLA BEAN BUTTER. Split 2 vanilla bean pods down the center vertically and scrape the seeds into the softened butter and stir.

CRANBERRY-APRICOT BUTTER. Coarsely chop ⅓ cup dried cranberries and ⅓ cup dried apricots. Stir into the softened butter.

LEMON POPPY SEED BUTTER. Stir 2 teaspoons grated fresh lemon zest and 1 tablespoon plus 1 teaspoon poppy seeds into the softened butter.

RUM RAISIN BUTTER. Coarsely chop ½ cup raisins. Place in a small saucepan set over medium heat and add 3 tablespoons spiced rum. Heat for about 2 minutes, just until the rum begins to steam. Remove the pan from the heat, and let cool. Stir all of the raisins and most of the rum into the butter.

PUMPKIN PIE BUTTER. Stir ⅓ cup unsweetened pumpkin purée, 2 tablespoons maple syrup, and 1½ teaspoons pumpkin pie spice into the butter.

BOURBON-BLACKBERRY BUTTER. Coarsely chop ¾ cup fresh blackberries. Toss with 1 tablespoon honey and 2 tablespoons bourbon. Stir into the softened butter.

HOT COCOA AND MARSHMALLOW FLUFF BUTTER. Melt ¾ cup dark chocolate chips. Let cool. Stir into the softened butter along with 1 tablespoon plus 1 teaspoon unsweetened cocoa powder. Fold in ¾ cup marshmallow fluff, leaving large streaks of marshmallow fluff throughout the butter.

Hot Cocoa and
Marshmallow Fluff

Parsley-Lemon-Chili

Bourbon-
Blackberry

Vanilla Bean

Pumpkin Pie

Cranberry-Apricot

BANANA BREAD GRANOLA

MAKES ABOUT 4 CUPS

Granola and banana bread, separately, are easy crowd pleasers, so it seemed obvious (to me) to combine them. This granola recipe bakes up in big batches and can be jarred and stored for weeks, if not eaten by the handful first. I like to use dehydrated banana slices in this recipe, as they're softer and more tender than crisp banana chips. If you prefer them crisp, banana chips are the way to go. Either way, this is a fragrant and comforting granola that is lovely served with tart Greek yogurt.

2½ cups old-fashioned oats

1 cup coarsely chopped pecans

½ cup flaxseed meal

¼ cup packed light brown sugar

1 teaspoon ground cinnamon

½ teaspoon freshly grated nutmeg

¼ teaspoon salt

½ cup pure maple syrup

⅓ cup melted coconut oil

2 teaspoons pure vanilla extract

1 cup unsweetened coconut flakes

2 cups dehydrated or dried banana slices

1. Place a rack in the upper third of the oven and preheat to 325°F. Line a rimmed baking sheet with parchment paper.

2. In a large bowl, combine the oats, pecans, flaxseed meal, brown sugar, cinnamon, nutmeg, and salt.

3. In a small bowl, whisk together the maple syrup, coconut oil, and vanilla. Pour the mixture into the oat mixture and stir well. Spread in a single layer on the prepared baking sheet.

4. Bake for 30 minutes, stirring every 10 minutes. Stir in the coconut flakes during the last 10 minutes of baking. Remove the pan from the oven and let the granola cool completely on the pan.

5. Once cool, toss in the dehydrated bananas. Store the granola for up to 2 weeks at room temperature in a large jar with an airtight lid.

PEACHES AND CREAM WITH
HONEYED CORNFLAKES

SERVES 4

These honeyed cornflakes are a slightly sticky play on granola. It's delicate but makes a statement. I love the simplicity and crunch from both cornflakes and almonds. Peaches and tart plain yogurt make excellent bedfellows for the honeyed cornflakes. These crunchy bites are also absolutely delicious served with Vanilla Rosemary Yogurt (page 144).

4 tablespoons unsalted butter

¼ cup plus 2 tablespoons honey

Pinch of salt

2 cups cornflakes, partially crushed

½ cup sliced almonds

1 tablespoon sesame seeds

2 cups plain Greek yogurt

2 ripe peaches, pitted and thinly sliced

1. Place a rack in the upper third of the oven and preheat to 325°F. Line a rimmed baking sheet with parchment paper and lightly grease the paper.

2. In a medium saucepan set over medium heat, combine the butter, ¼ cup of honey, and salt. Cook, stirring, for 4 to 6 minutes, until bubbling. Remove the pan from the heat and quickly stir in the cornflakes, almonds, and sesame seeds. Stir until everything is coated in honey and butter. Spread onto the prepared baking sheet.

3. Bake for 10 to 12 minutes, until golden. Let cool completely on the pan.

4. In a small bowl, stir together the yogurt and remaining 2 tablespoons honey. Divide the yogurt among four bowls and top with the peach slices and crunchy cornflake mixture to serve.

SANDWICHES

AND SALADS

What I want from a good breakfast sandwich is very simple. I want it cheesy, eggy, stacked high with crisp bacon, and wrapped in grease-stained paper for portability, even if that portability is only from plate to face. I think that there are two main types of breakfast sandwiches. There are those classy, pinkie-up, buttermilk-biscuit, platter-served bites perfect for late-morning brunches with tea and mimosas. Then there are greasy paper-wrapped egg-filled ones served with too-spicy micheladas late in the afternoon, when everyone (somehow, still) has bed head. Pick your brunch and pick your sandwich accordingly.

Now, I don't think anyone ever stretched their arms over their head when they woke up in the morning and instantly craved a big salad. That sounds suspicious at best. But salads fit in well among this ample gathering of sandwiches. They add a freshness that's often necessary at the brunch table among the richer dishes. To make a salad brunchworthy, I often add eggs or fresh fruit.

While sandwiches and salads can notoriously fall under the lunch category, we're standing firmly in brunch territory. When in doubt, add more bacon, poach an egg, and serve it all with mimosas.

BACON, BRIE, AND APPLE
GRILLED CHEESE

MAKES 4 SANDWICHES

Add Brie to any situation, and you've instantly elevated the dish from casual to elegant, even if it's just a grilled cheese sandwich. With crisp bacon and bright fresh apple slices, this sandwich is undeniably delicious. (See photograph, page 152.)

1. Heat a large cast-iron or nonstick skillet over medium heat.

2. Spread both sides of each slice of bread with butter. Top each slice of bread with a thick piece of Brie. Place two half slices of bacon on each of four pieces of bread. Top the bacon with up to four thin apple slices. Sprinkle lightly with pepper and top with the remaining bread slices.

3. Working with one or two sandwiches at a time, cook for about 3 minutes per side, until golden brown on the outside and the cheese is melted inside. Let cool for 5 minutes before cutting in half and serving.

8 slices sourdough bread

Clarified Butter (page 57), softened

8 thick slices Brie cheese, rind and all

4 slices cooked bacon, cut in half

1 Granny Smith apple, thinly sliced

Freshly cracked black pepper

THE BREAKFAST BURGER

It is an undisputed, very unscientific fact that a breakfast burger—of the fatty, greasy, almost overwhelming sort—is the best cure for a hangover. It seems that the answer to last night's overindulgence is a morning of overindulgence, right? There are healing powers hidden within the fat and carbs of this burger. Serve with a side of Hearts of Palm Fries (page 132), and just like that, we're cured of most everything, hangover and otherwise.

1. **FOR THE SAUCE:** In a small bowl, whisk together the mayonnaise, ketchup, mustard, salt, and pepper. Refrigerate until you're ready to assemble the burgers.

2. **FOR THE BURGERS:** Line a rimmed baking sheet with parchment paper and set to the side. In a medium bowl, combine the beef, sausage, Worcestershire sauce, garlic powder, salt, and pepper. Using your hands, mix well. Shape into six 4-ounce patties that are about 4 inches in diameter and place them on the prepared baking sheet. Cover and refrigerate at least 30 minutes.

3. Heat 1 tablespoon of oil in a large cast-iron skillet or stovetop griddle set over medium-high heat. Remove the burgers from the oven and cook three at a time, pressing with the back of a spatula, to your desired doneness—about 4 minutes per side for medium. In the last minute of cooking, top each patty with a slice of cheese. Transfer the burgers to a plate. Add the remaining oil to the pan and repeat with the remaining patties.

4. Split the buns and spread both sides with the sauce. Put the cheeseburgers on the bottom halves of the buns. Top each with a fried egg, 2 bacon pieces, a slice of tomato, lettuce, and the top of the bun.

SAUCE

½ cup mayonnaise

3 tablespoons ketchup

I tablespoon Dijon mustard

Sea salt

Freshly cracked black pepper

BURGERS

I pound 80% lean ground beef

½ pound spicy Italian sausage, casings removed

2 tablespoons Worcestershire sauce

½ teaspoon garlic powder

¾ teaspoon sea salt

I teaspoon freshly cracked black pepper

2 tablespoons canola oil

6 slices sharp cheddar cheese

6 brioche buns, toasted

6 fried eggs (see page 58)

6 slices cooked bacon, cut in half

6 thick tomato slices

6 whole iceberg lettuce leaves

BREAKFAST BLTS

MAKES 4 SANDWICHES

This breakfast BLT is the epitome of easy brunch fare. It combines toast, eggs, bacon, and even a few crisp vegetables for good measure. I think these sandwiches are best wrapped in waxed paper, packed to go, with a thermos of coffee and taken on a picnic. I challenge you not to gobble them in the car on the way.

8 thick slices bacon

⅓ cup mayonnaise

2 tablespoons Dijon mustard

Freshly cracked black pepper

8 thick slices white bread, toasted

4 slices cheddar or Swiss cheese

4 slices tomato

4 iceberg lettuce leaves

4 large fried eggs (see page 58)

1. Place racks in the upper third and center of the oven and preheat to 375°F.

2. Line a rimmed baking sheet with foil and arrange the bacon in a single layer. Bake for 15 to 18 minutes, until cooked through and crisp. Transfer to a paper towel–lined plate to drain and cool. Cut each piece of bacon in half.

3. In a small bowl, stir together the mayonnaise, mustard, and a few good pinches of pepper.

4. To assemble the sandwiches, line up the slices of bread on a work surface. Spread each slice with the mayonnaise mixture. Place a slice of cheese on four of the bread slices. Arrange four pieces of the bacon on each of the remaining four slices of bread. Top the cheese halves with tomato and lettuce. Top the bacon halves with a fried egg. Close up the sandwiches, cut in halves or quarters if desired, and serve.

FRENCH TOAST
HAM AND CHEESE SANDWICHES

SERVES 4

I have to admit that, in my heart, I'm somewhat of a breakfast purist. Put a plate of scrambled eggs and toast (burnt, because I always burn toast) in front of me, and I'm a happy camper. But brunch calls for a bit more indulgence, and that's why I love it! This sandwich is a decadent play on the classic Monte Cristo. For this version, instead of simple bread, I make a slice of French toast and pile everything on it in an over-the-top style.

1. **FOR THE FRENCH TOAST:** In a medium, shallow bowl, whisk together the eggs, milk, sugar, salt, and nutmeg.

2. In a nonstick skillet set over medium heat, melt a bit of clarified butter, just enough to coat the bottom of the pan. Dip a slice of brioche into the egg mixture, and let it rest for about 15 seconds on each side before transferring it to the hot pan. Cook for about 2 minutes per side, until golden brown on both sides. Transfer to a wire rack. Repeat with the remaining bread slices.

3. **FOR THE SANDWICHES:** Preheat the broiler.

4. Spread each slice of warm French toast with as much Dijon mustard as you'd like. Top each piece with three slices of ham and sprinkle with Gruyère. Place on a baking sheet.

5. Broil for about 2 minutes, until the ham is toasted and the cheese is bubbling and melted. Keep an eye on the sandwiches; they burn quickly. Serve warm.

FRENCH TOAST
3 large eggs
½ cup whole milk
I tablespoon sugar
Pinch of salt
Pinch of freshly grated nutmeg
Clarified Butter (page 57), for the pan
4 thick slices brioche

SANDWICHES
Dijon mustard
12 very thin ham slices
I cup finely grated Gruyère cheese

FRIED CHICKEN AND MAPLE
WAFFLE SANDWICHES

SERVES 6

There's a whole new bread category in the brunch realm. Between the hours of 10 a.m. and 2 p.m., waffles and pancakes become more than a foundation for a deep pool of syrup. All things that are carb-loaded and come from a griddle can be considered sandwich bread. Hallelujah! This might be the best thing to happen to fried chicken since sliced bread. See what I did there? See?

1. **FOR THE WAFFLES:** In a medium bowl, whisk together the flour, baking powder, baking soda, salt, and pepper.

2. In a small bowl, whisk together the eggs, maple syrup, butter, and buttermilk. Pour the mixture all at once into the flour mixture and whisk well. Let rest while you preheat the waffle iron.

3. When the waffle iron is hot, scoop ¼-cup portions into each of the quarters. Cook according to the manufacturer's instructions until golden brown. Transfer to a wire rack to cool. Repeat with the remaining batter. You should end up with twelve small waffles.

4. **FOR THE CHICKEN:** Season both sides of the chicken pieces with salt and pepper.

5. In a medium bowl, stir together the buttermilk, hot sauce, and onion slices. Add the chicken pieces and let marinate for 30 minutes.

6. In a separate medium bowl, whisk together the flour, garlic powder, 1 teaspoon salt, and 1 teaspoon pepper.

7. In a medium saucepan fitted with a deep-fry thermometer and set over medium heat, heat about 2 inches of oil to 350°F. Line a rimmed baking sheet with parchment paper and set aside.

WAFFLES

1½ cups all-purpose flour

¾ teaspoon baking powder

¾ teaspoon baking soda

¾ teaspoon salt

¾ teaspoon freshly cracked black pepper

2 large eggs

¼ cup pure maple syrup

4 tablespoons unsalted butter, melted and cooled

1½ cups buttermilk

CHICKEN

3 boneless, skinless chicken breasts, cut in half

Sea salt

Freshly cracked black pepper

2 cups buttermilk

1 tablespoon hot sauce

1 small onion, peeled and sliced

2 cups all-purpose flour

1 teaspoon garlic powder

Canola oil, for frying

8. Just before frying, remove a chicken piece from the buttermilk and let any excess buttermilk drain. Dredge both sides in the flour mixture and immediately lower the chicken piece into the hot oil. Cook three to four pieces of chicken at a time, and fry for about 7 minutes total, until cooked through and golden brown on both sides. Transfer to the prepared baking sheet. Repeat with the remaining chicken pieces.

9. **FOR THE SANDWICHES**: In a small bowl, combine the mayonnaise, mustard, maple syrup, and pepper. Spread the waffles with the mayonnaise mixture. Top 6 of the waffles with fried chicken, a tomato slice, and a piece of lettuce. Top each with another waffle, spear with a toothpick, and enjoy!

SANDWICHES

½ cup mayonnaise

2 tablespoons Dijon mustard

1 tablespoon pure maple syrup

½ teaspoon freshly cracked black pepper

2 tomatoes, sliced

6 iceberg lettuce leaves

MINI HAM AND BOURBON-PEACH
JAM BISCUITS

MAKES 18 TO 20 SANDWICHES

It's hard to decide sometimes what to put between the halves of a warm buttermilk biscuit. Salted butter is more than appropriate, and often it feels like anything more would be gilding the lily. But brunch is all about gilded lilies. These two-bite biscuits are layered with thinly sliced ham and slathered with a bourbon-infused peach jam, making them the Southern belle of any brunch table.

1. Place a rack in the upper third of the oven and preheat to 400°F. Line a rimmed baking sheet with parchment paper and set aside.

2. **FOR THE BISCUITS:** In a small bowl or liquid measuring cup, beat together the egg and buttermilk.

3. In a medium bowl, sift together the flour, sugar, baking powder, baking soda, and salt. Using your fingers, quickly work the butter into the mixture until some bits of butter are the size of oat flakes and some are the size of small peas. Create a well in the center of the flour mixture and add the egg mixture all at once. Stir into a shaggy mixture. The dough will be moist but not overly wet.

4. Turn the dough out onto a lightly floured work surface and, using a floured rolling pin, gently roll the dough into a 1-inch-thick oval. At the short end of the dough closest to you, fold the dough over until the edge meets the center of the dough. Fold the top edge toward the center and over the first fold. Gently roll the dough into a 1-inch oval and repeat the folding process twice more. Roll the dough out again to a 1-inch thickness. Using a 1½-inch round biscuit cutter (or the top of a small glass), cut out the biscuits.

BISCUITS

I large egg, lightly beaten

¾ cup cold buttermilk

3 cups all-purpose flour, plus more for rolling

2 tablespoons sugar

2½ teaspoons baking powder

½ teaspoon baking soda

¾ teaspoon salt

¾ cup high-quality, salted butter (like Plugrá), chilled and cut into small cubes, plus 2 tablespoons melted butter for brushing

JAM

8 ounces good-quality peach preserves

I tablespoon bourbon

I tablespoon honey

½ teaspoon grated fresh lemon zest

I teaspoon fresh lemon juice

10 slices country ham, cut in half or thirds

(recipe continues)

Reroll the dough scraps and cut out a few more biscuits. Place them 1 inch apart on the prepared baking sheet and brush lightly with melted butter.

5. Bake for 15 to 18 minutes, until golden brown on top. Transfer to a wire rack to cool slightly.

6. **FOR THE JAM**: In a small bowl, stir together the peach preserves, bourbon, honey, and lemon zest and juice.

7. To assemble the sandwiches, split the warm biscuits in half. Slather one side with the jam and top with 1 or 2 folded pieces of ham. Top each with a biscuit half and serve. These biscuits are best the day they're made.

FRIED GREEN TOMATO TOAST

MAKES 8 TOASTS

I had never had a delicious fried green tomato before moving to the Deep South. As far as I was concerned, it was the name of a film that I always got confused with *Driving Miss Daisy*. I had no idea that firm green tomatoes become succulent when fried up crisp. I like to pair them with a tangy ranch-style spread and make open-faced sandwiches, though they're great eaten fresh from the fryer.

1. **FOR THE YOGURT RANCH SPREAD:** In a small bowl, stir together the yogurt, buttermilk, chives, parsley, lemon juice, salt, and pepper. Taste and season as necessary. Refrigerate.

2. **FOR THE TOMATOES:** In a cast-iron skillet fitted with a deep-fry thermometer and set over medium heat, heat ¾ inch of canola oil to 375°F. (You may need to manually hold the thermometer bulb in the shallow oil for the temperature to register.)

3. Set three medium bowls next to the stove. Setup is key, because you'll need to work quickly. In one of the bowls, whisk together the flour, garlic powder, salt, and pepper. In another bowl, whisk together the eggs, buttermilk, and hot sauce. In the final bowl, combine the bread crumbs and cornmeal.

4. When the oil is hot, dip a tomato slice in the flour mixture. Dip it lightly in the egg mixture, and then dip it immediately in the panko mixture, lightly pressing to get the bread crumbs to stick. Place the tomato in the oil to fry, and repeat the process with three more tomato slices. Carefully flip and cook until golden, about 2 minutes on each side. Transfer to a paper towel–lined plate and sprinkle with a bit of coarse sea salt. Repeat with the remaining tomatoes.

5. Coat each slice of bread with the ranch spread. Top with tomato slices. Sprinkle with paprika, salt, and pepper, if desired.

YOGURT RANCH SPREAD

I cup full-fat Greek yogurt

3 tablespoons buttermilk

3 tablespoons chopped fresh chives

¼ cup coarsely chopped fresh parsley

I tablespoon fresh lemon juice

Sea salt

Freshly cracked black pepper

TOMATOES

Canola oil, for frying

I cup all-purpose flour

2 teaspoons garlic powder

I teaspoon sea salt, plus more for sprinkling

½ teaspoon freshly cracked black pepper, plus more for sprinkling

2 large eggs

½ cup buttermilk

Dash of Tabasco or your favorite hot sauce

2 cups panko bread crumbs, crushed well to a finer crumb

2 tablespoons cornmeal

2 large or 4 small green tomatoes, sliced thick

8 thick slices multigrain bread, toasted

Smoked paprika, for serving

MY FAVORITE
BREAKFAST SANDWICH

MAKES 6 SANDWICHES

This sandwich is the epitome of everything that recurs in my perfect breakfast dreams. I like to make these breakfast sandwiches on English muffins so all the nooks and crannies can catch the ketchup, mayonnaise, and sausage fat. Cheesy, salty, and beyond satisfying, this sandwich isn't called my favorite for nothing.

Spread the English muffins with as much ketchup, mayonnaise, and hot sauce as you'd like. Top with warm folded scrambled eggs, warm sausage patties, and the English muffin tops. Wrap in waxed paper so that it covers half of the sandwich (and presumably keeps your hands clean). Enjoy warm.

6 English muffins, split and lightly toasted

Ketchup

Mayonnaise

Your favorite hot sauce

6 Folded Scrambled Eggs (page 170)

6 Spicy Brown Sugar Sausage Patties (page 135)

FOLDED SCRAMBLED EGGS

My guilty pleasure foods usually cost around three dollars and are served from drive-through windows or over a deli counter in a grease-stained paper bag. Give me a McDonald's Sausage Egg and Cheese biscuit or an NYC-style egg and cheese bagel, and I'll likely kiss you on the mouth, whether you want me to or not. Lucky for both of us, this egg recipe is perfect for homemade versions of these indulgences. I adapted the easy and attainable method created by cooking genius Deb Perelman of Smitten Kitchen.

SERVES 1

I large egg

I teaspoon whole milk

Splash soy sauce or tamari

Freshly cracked black pepper

I teaspoon Clarified Butter (page 57)

2 tablespoons finely grated sharp cheddar cheese

1. In a small bowl, whisk together the egg, milk, soy sauce, and pepper.

2. In a 6-inch nonstick skillet set over medium heat, melt the clarified butter.

3. Pour the egg into the hot pan, tilting the pan to create a very thin, almost crepe-like layer. Reduce the heat to low and sprinkle the center 4-inch circle of egg with the cheese. Use a very thin spatula to fold the sides of the egg over the melting cheese, creating a small square. It's ready now, and won't last long, so slide it onto toast, into a sandwich, or something quickly and enjoy!

PASTRAMI AND RYE
GRILLED CHEESE WITH EGG

SERVES 4

It's hard to create a truly good deli sandwich at home, which really is what keeps good delis going strong. The combination of thinly sliced meat and melted cheese, along with the amount of fat they use on the griddle, can't be beat. I think there's also something about the waitress who is chewing gum and has an apron full of straws and pens as she brings you your perfect sandwich. This is my effort to bring that sandwich home, and I must say, it's pretty darn good.

4 tablespoons Clarified Butter (page 57), softened

8 slices rye bread

8 slices Swiss cheese

16 thin slices pastrami

4 fried eggs (see page 58)

1. Heat a griddle or nonstick skillet over medium heat.

2. Generously butter both sides of each slice of bread. Top each slice with Swiss cheese. Place two slices of pastrami on each slice of bread. Top four slices of bread with a fried egg, and close the sandwiches with the other.

3. Working with one or two sandwiches at a time, and pressing each sandwich with a spatula, cook for about 3 minutes per side, until golden brown on both sides and the cheese is melted inside. Let cool for 2 minutes before slicing in half and serving warm.

TEA SANDWICHES

For tea-type, pinkie-up, punch-bowl brunches, these pretty little sandwiches are just the thing. They're delicate but packed full of the deliciously complementary flavors of dill and smoked salmon. For a really lovely spread, serve them alongside Bacon and Deviled Eggs (page 66) and Blackberry Cobbler Muffins with Pistachios (page 217).

1. **FOR THE CREAM CHEESE SPREAD:** In a small bowl, combine the cream cheese, dill, chives, lemon juice and zest, salt, and pepper.

2. **FOR THE SANDWICHES:** Spread a thin layer of the cream cheese mixture on all of the bread slices. Layer slices of smoked salmon on the slices of whole-wheat bread. Top the salmon with a thin layer of arugula. Top with the white bread and press gently to seal. Cut the crusts off the sandwiches. Slice each sandwich into quarters, place on a platter, and serve. If you're not serving the sandwiches right away, cover with plastic wrap and refrigerate until ready to serve.

CREAM CHEESE SPREAD

8 ounces (1 package) cream cheese, at room temperature

1 tablespoon finely chopped fresh dill

1 tablespoon finely chopped fresh chives

2 tablespoons fresh lemon juice

1 teaspoon grated lemon zest

½ teaspoon sea salt

½ teaspoon freshly cracked black pepper

SANDWICHES

8 slices whole-wheat bread

8 slices white bread

1 (8-ounce) package sliced smoked salmon

2 heaping cups fresh arugula

FRIED SPAM AND EGG
BÁHN MÌ SANDWICHES

MAKES 4 SANDWICHES

Sure, New Orleans is famous for its beignets and Sazeracs; less well known is that it has some of the very best (and cheapest) báhn mì sandwiches, thanks to its booming Vietnamese population. I use SPAM in this sandwich, which isn't typical of my kitchen, but totally appropriate and delicious in this sandwich, and especially fantastic when paired with a fried egg. Piles of pickled vegetables, spicy jalapeño, and cilantro work to make this sandwich super fresh and incredibly delicious.

PICKLED CARROTS AND JALAPEÑO
½ cup white vinegar
½ cup water
2 tablespoons sugar
I teaspoon sea salt
I cup julienned carrots
I jalapeño, thinly sliced

SAUCE
½ cup mayonnaise
I heaping tablespoon Sriracha or other hot sauce
Dash of Worcestershire sauce
Freshly cracked black pepper

SANDWICHES
2 to 3 tablespoons canola oil
I can SPAM Classic, cold, drained, and cut into 8 slices
I fresh baguette, sliced into four 5-inch pieces and halved
4 large fried eggs (see page 58)
8 sprigs fresh cilantro
½ English cucumber, cut into 16 thin spears

1. **FOR THE PICKLED CARROTS AND JALAPEÑO:** In a small saucepan set over medium heat, combine the vinegar, water, sugar, and salt. Heat, stirring, for about 5 minutes, until the mixture is just steaming and the sugar is dissolved. Place the carrots and jalapeños in a small bowl and pour the warm vinegar mixture over the vegetables. Let cool to room temperature.

2. **FOR THE SAUCE:** In a small bowl, combine the mayonnaise, Sriracha, Worcestershire sauce, and pepper.

3. **FOR THE SANDWICHES:** In a medium skillet set over medium heat, heat 2 tablespoons of oil. Add the SPAM and cook for about 2 minutes per side, until light golden brown on both sides. Transfer to a paper towel–lined plate and let cool slightly.

4. Spread half of each baguette with the spicy mayonnaise and top with 2 slices of SPAM. Top with a fried egg. Drain the pickled carrots and jalapeños and pile on top of the fried eggs, followed by two sprigs of cilantro and four cucumber spears per sandwich.

THE GREEN GODDESS SANDWICH

MAKES 4 SANDWICHES

This vegetarian sandwich is in no way a shrinking violet. With loads of green vegetables and a bright herb mayonnaise, it is both light and satisfying. If you want to up the ante, substitute thick slices of buffalo mozzarella for the Havarti cheese, and if you must have meat, sliced turkey is a wonderful addition.

1. **FOR THE HERB MAYONNAISE:** In the bowl of a food processor fitted with the regular chopping blade, combine the mayonnaise, basil, chives, garlic, lemon zest and juice, and a good pinch of salt and pepper. Blend until smooth. Transfer to a small bowl and refrigerate until cold.

2. **FOR THE SANDWICHES:** Spread the herb mayonnaise onto each slice of bread. Make a thin, flat layer of avocado slices on four of the slices of bread. Add on layers of cucumber slices, spinach leaves, sprouts, and a slice of tomato. Top with cheese, if using, and top with the other four bread slices. Wrap each sandwich in waxed paper and slice in half, through the paper, just before serving. Keep chilled until ready to serve.

HERB MAYONNAISE

½ cup mayonnaise (or Greek yogurt)

Handful of fresh basil leaves

3 tablespoons finely chopped fresh chives

I small garlic clove

½ teaspoon grated lime zest

2 tablespoons fresh lime juice

Sea salt

Freshly cracked black pepper

SANDWICHES

8 thick slices whole-grain bread

I avocado, pitted and thinly sliced

I English cucumber, thinly sliced

2 heaping cups baby spinach leaves

2 heaping cups sprouts

I large green heirloom tomato

4 slices Havarti cheese (optional)

VEGAN BLACK BEAN
BREAKFAST TACOS

SERVES 4

During a visit to Austin, Texas, I discovered the wonders of the breakfast taco. I thought the taco would be the perfect way to explore the vegan side of breakfast, using onions, peppers, and loads of smoky spices to add flavor to tofu, which is very versatile. When crumbled and sautéed, firm tofu mimics scrambled eggs quite well. The black beans add extra protein, and fresh toppings give so much satisfaction.

1. **FOR THE SCRAMBLE:** In a medium skillet set over medium heat, heat the oil. Add the onion and bell pepper and cook, stirring occasionally, for 5 to 7 minutes, until soft and just beginning to brown. Add the tofu and cook, breaking up the tofu with the back of a wooden spoon, for about 8 minutes, until just beginning to brown.

2. In a small bowl, combine 2 tablespoons water with the chili powder, cumin, smoked paprika, garlic powder, salt, and pepper. Pour the spice mixture over the tofu mixture. Stir in the black beans, reduce the heat to low, and simmer for 5 minutes, until heated through.

3. In a nonstick skillet set over medium heat, heat the oil. Fry the tortillas one at a time, flipping once, until heated through, about 4 minutes. Transfer to a paper towel–lined plate to drain.

4. Place two tortillas on each of four plates. Divide the tofu scramble among the tortillas, and top with salsa, onions, cilantro, spinach, and jalapeños, as desired, and serve warm.

SCRAMBLE

2 tablespoons canola oil

½ cup chopped yellow onion

½ cup chopped red bell pepper

8 ounces firm tofu, drained and crumbled into large chunks

I teaspoon chili powder

I teaspoon ground cumin

½ teaspoon smoked paprika

½ teaspoon garlic powder

I teaspoon salt

½ teaspoon freshly cracked black pepper

I (15-ounce) can black beans, rinsed and drained

3 tablespoons canola oil

8 corn tortillas

TOPPINGS (optional)

Spicy salsa

Finely chopped yellow onion

Coarsely chopped fresh cilantro

Baby spinach leaves

Pickled jalapeños

CHICKEN AVOCADO AREPAS

SERVES 6 TO 8

Philadelphia wouldn't be the first place I'd expect to learn how to make arepas, a traditional Venezuelan dish—but sometimes food friends live in unexpected places. My friend Ilana taught me how to make these arepas in her tiny though thoroughly capable kitchen one Sunday afternoon. They are made with precooked white corn flour (I use Goya masarepa or maseca), which you can find in some grocery stores or online, pan-seared and then oven-baked, and I think of them as a cross between flatbread and tortillas. I like them warm with a cool and creamy chicken and avocado salad. I suggest that you make a double batch, invite many friends, and serve with micheladas (page 28).

1. **FOR THE SALAD:** In a medium bowl, roughly mash the avocados. Stir in the chicken, mayonnaise or yogurt, lime juice, onion, cilantro, garlic, jalapeños, salt, and pepper. Season with more salt, pepper, and/or lime juice to taste. Refrigerate for 1 hour, until cold.

2. **FOR THE AREPAS:** Place racks in the center and lower third of the oven and preheat to 350°F.

3. In a large bowl, whisk together the corn flour and salt. Add the boiled water and, using a wooden spoon, stir well. The mixture will become so thick that you may need to use your hands to knead it, working out any lumps. Cover with a kitchen towel and let rest for 5 minutes.

4. Place the dough on a clean work surface and divide it into 8 or 10 pieces.

SALAD

3 ripe Hass avocados, peeled and pitted

4 cups Poached Chicken (recipe follows)

4 tablespoons mayonnaise or Greek yogurt

Juice of 2 limes

¼ cup finely chopped white onion

¼ cup coarsely chopped fresh cilantro

I garlic clove, minced

½ jalapeño, seeded and finely chopped

½ teaspoon sea salt, plus more as needed

½ teaspoon freshly cracked black pepper, plus more as needed

AREPAS

3 cups precooked white corn flour

I teaspoon sea salt

3 to 3½ cups boiled water

Canola oil, for the pan

5. Heat a cast-iron or nonstick skillet over medium heat. Add just enough oil to cover the bottom of the pan. Place three arepas in the skillet and cook for about 4 minutes per side, until browned on each side. Transfer the arepas directly onto the wire racks of the oven. Repeat with the remaining arepa dough.

6. Bake the arepas for 10 to 12 minutes, until they are lightly puffed and sound a bit hollow when tapped. Keep an eye on the arepas as they'll cook and bake in batches.

7. Transfer the arepas to a wire rack and let cool. Slice through half of each arepa (as you might cut through a pita) and stuff it with the chicken and avocado salad. Serve immediately.

POACHED CHICKEN

MAKES ABOUT 4 CUPS SHREDDED CHICKEN

In a medium saucepan set over medium heat, add the chicken and enough stock to cover it. Add the bay leaf and peppercorns and bring to a simmer. Reduce the heat to low, cover, and simmer for 10 to 14 minutes, until the chicken is cooked through. Transfer the chicken to a plate and let cool. When the chicken is cool enough to handle, shred it into bite-size pieces.

1 pound boneless, skinless chicken breast

Chicken stock

1 bay leaf

5 whole black peppercorns

THE BREAKFAST BURRITO

SERVES 8

I got through shooting the photographs for my last cookbook for two reasons: my photographer and friend Jon Melendez and his near-constant delivery of breakfast burritos. He'd stop at our favorite hole-in-the-wall, pick up potato-egg-bacon burritos, and drive them out to the little bungalow in Venice where we would shoot the cookbook, eat burritos, and try to wrangle my giant cat. This is an homage to those beautiful days.

1. Fill a medium saucepan with cool water and add the potato quarters. Salt the water, bring to a simmer over medium heat, and cook until the potatoes are cooked through, about 15 minutes. Drain the potatoes in a colander and let cool slightly.

2. In a large skillet set over medium heat, heat the oil. Add the onions and bell pepper. Cook, stirring occasionally, for 5 to 7 minutes, until soft and beginning to brown. Add the jalapeños and cook for 3 more minutes. Season with sea salt and pepper.

3. When the potatoes are cool enough to handle, cut them into bite-size pieces and add them to the pan with the onions and the peppers. Cook, stirring, for about 5 minutes, until the potatoes are slightly browned. Remove the pan from the heat.

4. In a small bowl, mash together the avocado and lemon juice. Mix in sea salt to taste.

5. Wrap the tortillas in two moist paper towels. Microwave for 20 seconds to soften.

6. Into each tortilla, layer the potatoes, scrambled eggs, bacon, a dollop of avocado, a sprinkling of cheese, and some salsa. Fold the bottom and the top of the tortilla over and roll from the sides. Wrap in foil or waxed paper and serve.

2 large russet potatoes, cut into quarters

Salt, for the cooking water

2 tablespoons canola oil

I medium yellow onion, chopped

I red bell pepper, seeded, and chopped

I small jalapeño, seeded and finely chopped

Sea salt

Freshly cracked black pepper

I ripe Hass avocado, peeled and pitted

I tablespoon fresh lemon juice

8 (9- to II-inch) flour tortillas

8 large scrambled eggs (see page 55)

8 slices cooked bacon, finely chopped

1½ cups shredded sharp cheddar cheese

½ cup spicy salsa

BREAKFAST QUESADILLAS
WITH SAUSAGE AND CHEESE

SERVES 2

In the never-ending quest to combine meat, starch, and cheese for breakfast, I bring you the breakfast quesadilla. The salty sausage, melt-y cheese, and pan-fried crunch of the tortilla combine many comforts especially for breakfast. Thankfully, these quesadillas are also easy to assemble, even if you may have had three too many beers the night before. Incidentally, they are delicious served with micheladas (page 13). Hair of the dog. You're welcome.

1. In a medium skillet set over medium heat, cook the sausage meat, breaking it up with a spatula or wooden spoon, for about 8 minutes, until cooked through. Transfer to a small bowl.

2. In a separate small bowl, whisk together the eggs and a pinch of salt and pepper. In the same skillet used for the sausage, set over medium heat, warm 1 tablespoon of oil. Add the eggs and cook, stirring occasionally, for 5 to 7 minutes, until solid and cooked through. Transfer the eggs to a bowl. Clean the skillet and return it to medium-low heat. Add the remaining tablespoon of oil.

3. Sprinkle 2 tortillas with half of the cheddar cheese. Divide the sausage and eggs between the 2 tortillas. Add the remaining cheddar cheese and top with the 2 remaining tortillas. Now you have quesadillas.

4. Add remaining oil to the pan and place one quesadilla in the pan and cook for about 3 minutes, until golden. Flip carefully and cook for about 3 more minutes, until golden brown on the second side. Repeat with second quesadilla. Slide cooked quesadillas onto a plate, slice into wedges, and serve warm with avocado, sour cream, Sriracha, and roasted cherry tomatoes.

2 mild Italian sausage links, casings removed

3 tablespoons canola oil

4 large eggs

Salt

Freshly cracked black pepper

4 medium flour tortillas

1½ cups coarsely grated cheddar cheese

1 ripe avocado, sliced

⅓ cup sour cream, for topping

Sriracha or your favorite hot sauce, for topping

Roasted Cherry Tomatoes (page 136), for serving

BOOK CLUB
CHICKEN SALAD

SERVES 6

Here's the deal with a ladies' book club. It's never really about the book. It's more about enjoying gossip, pink wine, and brunchy snacks, all under the guise of literary discussion. For this reason, it's essential that you join a book club with friends who know how to throw down in the kitchen, and that you perfect your signature book club dish. With deliciously moist chicken, sweet grapes, and intriguing curry powder, this chicken salad is your golden ticket.

1. In a large bowl, combine the chicken, grapes, apples, celery, almonds, and chives. Add the yogurt, mayonnaise, lemon juice, curry powder, salt, and pepper, and toss well. Refrigerate for at least 4 hours, though overnight is best; it should be chilled through.

2. Serve over salad greens or on toasted brioche.

4 cups Poached Chicken (page 181)

1 cup halved red grapes

1 cup chopped Granny Smith apples

1 cup thinly sliced celery

½ cup toasted sliced almonds

3 tablespoons finely chopped fresh chives

½ cup plain Greek yogurt

¼ cup mayonnaise

1 tablespoon fresh lemon juice

1 teaspoon curry powder

Sea salt

Freshly cracked black pepper

Salad greens or toasted brioche, for serving

BLUEBERRY-PISTACHIO TABBOULEH

SERVES 4

My parents were early adopters of health food. We're talking late 1970s-type health food, when tofu and the weirdest wild rices and gnarly grains were coming into fashion. I remember eating a lot of parsley-heavy tabbouleh, much to my five-year-old self's deep chagrin. This salad is an homage to my early health food memories, with modern additions of sweet blueberries and salty pistachios.

Salt, for the water

¾ cup bulgur wheat

I garlic clove, minced

3 scallions (both white and green parts), thinly sliced

I English cucumber, chopped

⅓ cup finely chopped fresh mint leaves

Heaping ½ cup finely chopped flat-leaf parsley

¼ cup olive oil

I tablespoon red wine vinegar

Zest and juice of I lemon

½ teaspoon sea salt, plus more as needed

I teaspoon freshly cracked black pepper, plus more as needed

½ teaspoon dried oregano

¼ teaspoon ground cinnamon

I cup fresh blueberries

½ cup shelled and coarsely chopped salted pistachios

½ cup crumbled sheep's milk feta (optional but delicious)

1. Rinse and drain the bulgur. Bring 1¼ cups water to a boil. Add a pinch of salt and the bulgur, cover, and remove the pan from the heat. Let sit for 25 to 30 minutes, until the liquid has absorbed. Uncover the pan and stir in the garlic. Set aside to cool (or transfer to a small bowl and put in the refrigerator).

2. Once the bulgur has cooled, transfer it to a large bowl. Add the scallions, cucumber, mint, and parsley, and toss well. Add the olive oil, vinegar, lemon zest and juice, salt, pepper, oregano, and cinnamon. Gently toss to combine. Add the blueberries and pistachios. Season with more salt and pepper to taste. Toss in the feta cheese, if using. Refrigerate until cold, about 1 hour, before serving. The salad will keep for 3 days in an airtight container in the refrigerator.

MUFFALETTA BRUNCH SALAD

SERVES 8

With the classic po'boy, the Vietnamese bánh mì, and the Italian muffaletta, New Orleans knows its way around a great sandwich. The classic muffaletta is a combination of chopped olive salad, salami, cheese, and vinaigrette pressed in Sicilian sesame bread. I've made the classic brunch-friendly by layering those familiar flavors in a pasta salad and adding hard-boiled eggs. It's best after a day in the refrigerator and is perfect for feeding a hungry crowd.

1. **FOR THE SALAD:** Bring a large pot of salted water to a boil and cook the pasta al dente, according to the package directions. Drain and transfer to a large bowl. Add the olive oil and garlic, toss well, and let cool to room temperature.

2. To the cooled pasta, add the onions, celery, parsley, dried oregano, dried basil, and celery seed, and toss well.

3. Cut the salami, ham, turkey, and cheese into small cubes and add to the pasta. Add the eggs and the black and green olives. Season with salt and pepper and toss well.

4. **FOR THE VINAIGRETTE:** In a jar with a tight-fitting lid, combine the olive oil, vinegar, Worcestershire sauce, hot sauce to taste, and salt and pepper. Place the lid on the jar and shake vigorously. Taste and add more salt and pepper as desired. Drizzle three-quarters of the vinaigrette over the pasta salad and toss. Cover and refrigerate for at least 8 hours, or overnight. Toss with the remaining vinaigrette and sprinkle with Parmesan cheese just before serving.

SALAD

Salt, for the water

1 pound cooked pasta shells

2 tablespoons olive oil

1 large garlic clove, minced

1 small yellow onion, finely chopped

4 celery stalks, chopped

1/2 cup chopped fresh parsley

2 tablespoons dried oregano

1 tablespoon dried basil

1 teaspoon celery seed

4 1/4-inch-thick slices dry salami

3 1/4-inch-thick slices boiled ham

3 1/4-inch-thick slices roasted turkey

3 1/4-inch-thick slices provolone cheese

4 hard-boiled eggs (see page 62), peeled and sliced

1 cup sliced black olives

1 cup sliced green olives

Freshly cracked black pepper

VINAIGRETTE

3/4 cup olive oil

1/3 cup apple cider vinegar

2 teaspoons Worcestershire sauce

Hot sauce

Sea salt

Freshly cracked black pepper

Shredded Parmesan cheese, for serving

STRAWBERRY CITRUS SALAD
WITH WHIPPED CRÈME FRAÎCHE

SERVES 6

Bruised banana slices and browning apple slices have no place on our elegant brunch table. When it comes to fruit salads, opt instead for ripe strawberries and citrus rounds combined with unexpected herbal notes. Tarragon is an herb that has a subtle licorice flavor that pairs beautifully with sweet fruit.

1. **FOR THE SALAD:** In a medium bowl, combine the strawberries, 3 tablespoons of the sugar, and the tarragon. Cover and let sit for 20 minutes, until the berries have released some of their juices.

2. To prepare the grapefruit, blood orange, and navel orange, slice off the top and bottom of each of the fruits, creating a base. Stand the fruit up on the base and slice off the peel and pith from around the fruit. Slice the fruit into ¼-inch-thick rounds. Put the citrus in a large bowl. Add the tangerine segments and strawberry mixture. Refrigerate for 30 minutes.

3. **FOR THE WHIPPED CRÈME FRAÎCHE:** In the bowl of a stand mixer fitted with the whisk attachment, beat the cream, confectioners' sugar, and salt on medium speed for about 5 minutes, until the cream holds soft peaks. Remove the bowl from the mixer and, using a spatula, fold in the crème fraîche, using a whisk to aerate.

4. To serve, divide the fruit among six small bowls and spoon some juice over the fruit. Dollop with whipped crème fraîche and top with a tarragon sprig.

SALAD

I pound fresh strawberries, hulled and sliced

½ cup plus 3 tablespoons granulated sugar

2 tablespoons coarsely chopped fresh tarragon, plus 6 sprigs for garnish

I pink grapefruit

2 blood oranges

2 navel oranges

2 seedless tangerines, peeled and segmented

WHIPPED CRÈME FRAÎCHE

I cup heavy cream

2 tablespoons confectioners' sugar

Pinch of salt

¼ cup crème fraîche, at room temperature

SPINACH, BLUEBERRY, AND AVOCADO
SALAD

SERVES 6

———————————●———————————

Some brunch dishes are an elegant smash-bang (the most elegant of words) of breakfast moments and lunch elements. This salad, with its fresh blueberries, toasted hazelnuts, and honey dressing, brings sweetness to a savory spinach salad. If you don't have blueberries on hand, sliced strawberries would also be delicious!

1. **FOR THE DRESSING:** In a small bowl, whisk together the honey, mustard, and good pinches of salt and pepper. Whisk in the lemon juice. Whisking constantly, slowly drizzle in the oil until the mixture is emulsified and thick. Season with salt and pepper to taste.

2. **FOR THE SALAD:** In a large bowl, toss together the spinach, blueberries, cucumber, avocado, and hazelnuts, reserving some avocado and hazelnuts for topping. Drizzle as much dressing as you'd like over the salad and toss well. Top with the remaining avocado and hazelnuts, season with salt and pepper, and serve.

DRESSING

2 tablespoons honey

1 tablespoon Dijon mustard

Sea salt

Freshly cracked black pepper

Juice of 1 lemon

¼ cup olive oil

SALAD

6 heaping cups baby spinach

1 cup fresh blueberries

1 heaping cup thinly sliced English cucumber

1 ripe avocado, peeled, pitted, and thinly sliced

⅓ cup coarsely chopped toasted hazelnuts

Salt

Freshly cracked black pepper

BAKED GOODS

Perhaps one of the best features of brunch is the acceptability of cake at breakfast. More than acceptable, cake is encouraged. Whether blueberry-studded or dripping in pecans and caramel, as long as it's served alongside a cup of coffee, it's a perfectly acceptable before-noon endeavor.

Some breakfast baked goods are both sweet and savory. Some tread lightly into sweetness, incorporating lots of fresh fruit into our morning pastries. (The fruit in that cupcake really just makes it a muffin, right?) Other recipes, like the Chocolate Hazelnut Coffee Cake (page 221), are downright desserts, giving new meaning to the phrase "Always have dessert first." I'm hoping that suggestion was intended to mean, "Just go ahead and have your dessert with your morning coffee."

These recipes are meant to be shared and ogled, piled high on a platter, and dripped to excess with glaze. They're meant to make your guests' hearts skip a beat. Sure, that's a lot. Yes, I realize this is just breakfast. But it's *not* just breakfast, it's a beautiful brunch, our moment to pause in hectic schedules and enjoy a much smaller universe, where friends, laughter, morning cocktails, and huge cinnamon rolls are the only things that matter.

Now, if we could only find a way to have ice cream at breakfast, too, we'd really be doing things right.

BAKED BROWN-BUTTER
BANANA BREAD DOUGHNUTS

MAKES 24 TO 28 DOUGHNUTS

Because we're brunching, classic banana bread can't just loaf around. So I've transformed the buttery, sweet, comforting bread into baked doughnuts. Same bread, clever shape. The trick with these treats is to only fill the doughnut pan to just over half full. If you overfill, you'll lose the hole in the center, turning them into hockey pucks. Yes, this recipe does call for a new baking pan, but once you realize all of the other recipes you can finagle into a doughnut shape, life gets a little more precious.

1. Place a rack in the center of the oven and preheat to 350°F. Grease two mini doughnut pans with nonstick cooking spray. Line a rimmed baking sheet with parchment paper.

2. **FOR THE CRUMB TOPPING:** In a medium bowl, whisk together the flour, sugars, cinnamon, and salt. Add the butter and, using your fingers, quickly blend the butter into the flour mixture until there are bits the size of oat flakes but most is incorporated into the mixture. Spread into an even layer on the prepared baking sheet. Bake for 18 to 20 minutes, stirring twice during baking, until lightly brown. Let cool completely.

3. **FOR THE DOUGHNUTS:** In a large bowl, whisk together the flour, sugar, baking soda, cinnamon, nutmeg, and salt.

4. In a medium bowl, whisk together the browned butter, eggs, vanilla, and buttermilk. Whisk in the mashed bananas. Add the mixture all at once to the flour mixture. Fold together, making sure to scrape the bottom of the bowl to get hidden pockets of flour, until just combined; do not overwork. Spoon the batter into the prepared doughnut pan.

CRUMB TOPPING
1¼ cups all-purpose flour

½ cup lightly packed light brown sugar

½ cup granulated sugar

1½ teaspoons ground cinnamon

¼ teaspoon salt

½ cup (1 stick) unsalted butter, cold and cut into small cubes

DOUGHNUTS
2 cups all-purpose flour

¾ cup granulated sugar

1 teaspoon baking soda

¾ teaspoon ground cinnamon

½ teaspoon freshly grated nutmeg

½ teaspoon salt

½ cup Browned Butter, cooled slightly (page 97)

2 large eggs

1 teaspoon pure vanilla extract

¼ cup buttermilk

1¼ cups mashed banana (from about 3 medium bananas)

GLAZE
2 cups confectioners' sugar

Pinch of salt

3 tablespoons unsalted butter, melted

1 teaspoon pure vanilla extract

3 to 4 tablespoons whole milk

(recipe continues)

5. Bake for 12 to 15 minutes, until a toothpick inserted in a doughnut comes out clean. Let cool in the pan for 5 minutes before inverting onto a wire rack to cool completely.

6. **FOR THE GLAZE**: In a medium bowl, whisk together the confectioners' sugar and salt. Whisk in the butter, vanilla, and 2 tablespoons of milk. Add more milk, if needed, for a thin and very spreadable consistency.

7. Once the doughnuts are completely cool, use a butter knife to spread each doughnut with glaze and immediately add a generous amount of crumble topping to each doughnut. Let set for 15 minutes before serving. The doughnuts are best the day they're made, but they will keep for up to 3 days in an airtight container at room temperature.

ALMOND CRUMBLE
COFFEE CAKE MUFFINS

MAKES 12 MUFFINS

I think almond extract is what sprinkles out of magic wands when the kitchen fairies come in to work their magic. Even just a splash of it transforms a basic muffin into a sophisticated, classy accompaniment to milky tea (served in delicate teacups, of course). This muffin recipe is versatile; try adding blueberries or chopped strawberries.

1. Place a rack in the upper third of the oven and preheat to 350°F. Line a twelve-cup muffin tin with liners.

2. **FOR THE CRUMBLE**: In a medium bowl, whisk together the flour, brown sugar, cinnamon, nutmeg, and salt. Add the butter and, using your fingers, quickly rub it into the dry ingredients. Some butter pieces will be in large bits; that's great. Set aside.

3. **FOR THE MUFFINS**: In a medium bowl, whisk together the browned butter, sour cream, egg, egg yolk, and vanilla and almond extracts.

4. In a separate medium bowl, whisk together the flour, sugar, baking powder, and salt. Add to the butter mixture and stir gently to combine. Spoon half of the batter into the muffin cups. Sprinkle 1 heaping tablespoon of crumble into each cup, and then top with the remaining batter. Sprinkle another tablespoon of crumble on top of each muffin, and sprinkle each with chopped almonds. Using a knife, gently swirl the crumble into each muffin.

5. Bake for 18 to 20 minutes, until golden brown; a toothpick inserted into the center of a muffin should come out with just a few moist crumbs. Transfer the pan to a wire rack and let cool for 15 minutes before removing the muffins from the pan. The muffins are best served warm the day they are made, but they'll keep for up to 4 days well wrapped at room temperature.

CRUMBLE

½ cup all-purpose flour

½ cup lightly packed light brown sugar

I teaspoon ground cinnamon

½ teaspoon freshly grated nutmeg

½ teaspoon salt

¼ cup (½ stick) cold unsalted butter, cut into pieces

MUFFINS

½ cup Browned Butter (page 97)

½ cup sour cream

I large egg plus I large egg yolk

I teaspoon pure vanilla extract

½ teaspoon pure almond extract

1¾ cups all-purpose flour

¾ cup granulated sugar

I½ teaspoons baking powder

½ teaspoon salt

⅓ cup roasted almonds, finely chopped, for topping

MINI APRICOT AND CARDAMOM
SCONES

MAKES 20 TO 24 SCONES

Perfectly ripe, sweet, and soft apricots are like unicorns in the fruit world. They're hard to come by unless you live directly under an apricot tree. When you find them, buy them by the armful, hoard them as necessary, and make everything from these scones to jam. If you can't find any good fresh ones, plump dried apricots (first rehydrated in a bit of water and orange juice) will work great instead.

3 cups all-purpose flour, plus more for kneading

⅓ cup sugar, plus more for sprinkling

I tablespoon baking powder

½ teaspoon ground cardamom

I teaspoon salt

I½ cups heavy cream, plus more for brushing

I teaspoon pure vanilla extract

¾ cup coarsely chopped fresh apricots

1. Place a rack in the upper third of the oven and preheat to 425°F. Line a rimmed baking sheet with parchment paper.

2. In a medium bowl, whisk together the flour, sugar, baking powder, cardamom, and salt.

3. In a liquid measuring cup combine the cream and vanilla. Pour the cream mixture into the flour mixture, tossing and stirring as you go. Toss in the apricot chunks, stirring to create a cohesive, but not sticky dough.

4. Place the dough on a lightly floured work surface. Gently gather and knead the dough, and press it into a ¾-inch-thick disk. Using a small (1¼-inch) biscuit cutter (or the top of a small glass), cut circles out of the dough and transfer them to the prepared baking sheet. Brush each circle with heavy cream and sprinkle generously with sugar.

5. Bake for 12 to 14 minutes, until golden brown and cooked through. Serve warm. Scones are best served the day they're made but will keep for up to 3 days at room temperature in an airtight container.

CHOCOLATE BRIOCHE
CINNAMON ROLLS

MAKES 12 ROLLS

Brioche is a beautiful dough. Smooth, supple, versatile, down for anything—it has all the shining, sexy qualities you hope your mate sees in you. Others may see just dough, but it really is special. Because this rich dough is so amiable, we're studding it with dark chocolate and filling it with a sweetly spiced cinnamon roll filling.

Bonus! This dough can be made—and even assembled—the evening before and stored, covered, in the refrigerator. Just bring the dough or rolls to room temperature before kneading or baking.

1. **FOR THE DOUGH:** In a small bowl, combine the warm water and yeast. Let it sit for 5 minutes, until foamy.

2. In a medium bowl, whisk together the eggs, butter, and honey.

3. In the bowl of a stand mixer fitted with a dough hook, combine the flour, salt, and nutmeg. Add the egg mixture and yeast mixture, and use a spatula to bring the ingredients together into a shaggy dough. Fit the bowl onto the mixer and mix on medium speed for 5 to 7 minutes, until the dough pulls away from the sides of the bowl. Add the chocolate and beat for 2 more minutes, until evenly combined. Cover the bowl in plastic wrap and let rest in a warm place until puffed and doubled in size, about 2 hours.

4. **FOR THE FILLING:** In a small bowl, toss together the sugar, cinnamon, nutmeg, and salt. Set aside.

5. Turn the risen dough out onto a lightly floured work surface. Using a floured rolling pin, roll the dough into a ½-inch-thick rectangle. Brush with the 4 tablespoons melted butter and sprinkle with the filling. Starting from the long end, tightly roll the dough into a log. Slice it into twelve equal pieces.

DOUGH

½ cup warm water

2½ teaspoons (1 package) active dry yeast

3 large eggs, at room temperature, lightly beaten

½ cup (1 stick) unsalted butter, melted and cooled slightly

¼ cup honey

4½ cups all-purpose flour, plus more for rolling

¾ teaspoon salt

¼ teaspoon freshly grated nutmeg

½ cup mini dark chocolate chips or finely chopped dark chocolate

FILLING

1 cup lightly packed light brown sugar

1 tablespoon plus 2 teaspoons ground cinnamon

½ teaspoon freshly grated nutmeg

Generous pinch of salt

4 tablespoons unsalted butter, melted

(recipe continues)

6. Generously butter a 9 × 13-inch pan. Place rolls in the prepared pan, cover with a kitchen towel, and let rise for 30 minutes.

7. Place a rack in the upper third of the oven and preheat to 350°F.

8. Bake until the rolls are risen, golden brown, and bubbling, 25 to 30 minutes. Let cool to a warm room temperature.

9. **FOR THE GLAZE**: Put the cream cheese into a bowl and microwave for about 10 seconds, until it is very soft. Transfer to the bowl of a stand mixer fitted with the paddle attachment. Add the butter and beat well. Add the confectioners' sugar, salt, vanilla, and a splash of milk. Beat until smooth and spreadable. Frost the rolls and serve.

10. The rolls are best fresh from the oven, but will keep for 3 days, well wrapped at room temperature.

GLAZE

1 (8-ounce) package cream cheese, at room temperature

4 tablespoons unsalted butter, at room temperature

2 cups confectioners' sugar

Pinch of salt

1 teaspoon pure vanilla extract

Splash of milk

OVERNIGHT NEW ORLEANS
BEIGNETS

MAKES ABOUT 36 BEIGNETS

Living in New Orleans, I've learned a thing or five about beignets, the little pockets of freshly fried dough that are indigenous to this city. Beignets should be piled sky-high, snowy with powdered sugar, and very, very, very fresh from the fryer. (It's nice to have friends gather around and enjoy them as they cook.) This recipe calls for the dough to rest in the refrigerator overnight, developing the flavor and allowing you to get your beauty sleep. Let the dough come to room temperature before shaping and frying, and be prepared for a light dusting of powdered sugar over everything in your kitchen.

2 tablespoons warm water (99°F to 105°F)

2½ teaspoons (1 package) active dry yeast

¼ cup plus a pinch of granulated sugar

½ cup warm Browned Butter (page 97)

1 cup whole milk, warmed slightly

1 large egg, lightly beaten

3½ to 4 cups all-purpose flour, plus more for rolling

1 teaspoon salt

½ teaspoon baking powder

Canola oil, for frying

6 cups confectioners' sugar

1. In the bowl of a stand mixer, whisk together the water, yeast, and a pinch of sugar. Let it rest for 5 minutes, until foamy. Add the browned butter, the warmed milk, ¼ cup sugar, and egg.

2. Add 2 cups of flour, the salt, and baking powder. Beat on low speed, adding more flour (up to 1½ to 2 cups more) until you have a soft, slightly sticky dough. Scrape down the sides of the bowl, sprinkle with a bit more flour, cover with plastic wrap, and let rest at room temperature for 30 minutes before placing in the refrigerator overnight.

3. In the morning, remove the dough from the refrigerator and let it sit at room temperature for 30 minutes.

4. Punch down the dough and dump it onto a lightly floured work surface. Roll the dough out into a roughly 16 × 12-inch rectangle and, using a pizza cutter, cut it into 2-inch squares. Cover lightly with plastic wrap.

(recipe continues)

5. In a medium saucepan fitted with a deep-fry thermometer and set over medium heat, heat about 2 inches of oil to 375°F.

6. Spread a generous amount of confectioners' sugar on a rimmed baking sheet. Working in batches of about four, gently lower the beignets into the hot oil and cook for 2 to 3 minutes total, until golden brown on each side. Using a slotted spoon, transfer them directly to the confectioners' sugar and toss immediately. Let the oil to return to 375°F before each batch and repeat with the remaining beignets. Serve immediately.

FIG AND PISTACHIO
BUTTERMILK CAKE

MAKES ONE 10-INCH SKILLET CAKE

Somewhere in my impressionable youth I decided that figs were horrible fruits meant solely to punish those who ate them. It probably had something to do with the whole-wheat fig bars my parents kept in the house as our only sweet treat—a sorry excuse for cookies and for figs. Thankfully, my eyes (and mouth) have been opened to the beauty of fresh figs. They're sweet, slightly crunchy, soft, really intricate fruits that absolutely shine atop this tender buttermilk cake.

I really enjoy toasted pistachios for added depth and texture in this cake. Leave them out if you'd like, or substitute toasted pecans or even roasted walnuts.

1. FOR THE CAKE: Place a rack in the center of the oven and preheat to 375°F. Butter and flour a 10-inch cast-iron skillet or a 10-inch round cake pan.

2. In a medium bowl, whisk together the flour, sugar, baking powder, baking soda, cardamom, and salt.

3. In a small bowl, whisk together the eggs, buttermilk, melted butter, and vanilla. Add the buttermilk mixture all at once to the flour mixture and stir until just combined. Spoon the batter into the prepared skillet or pan. Top with the fig halves, cut side up, gently pressing the figs partially into the batter. Sprinkle with chopped pistachios and then sprinkle generously with sugar.

4. Bake for 20 to 25 minutes, until a toothpick inserted in the center of the cake comes out clean. Let cool to room temperature before slicing and serving.

5. The cake will keep for up to 3 days, well wrapped in the refrigerator.

CAKE

¼ cup unsalted butter, melted and slightly cooled, plus more for the pan

2½ cups all-purpose flour, plus more for the pan

¾ cup granulated sugar

2 teaspoons baking powder

½ teaspoon baking soda

½ teaspoon ground cardamom

½ teaspoon salt

2 large eggs

1½ cups buttermilk

1 teaspoon pure vanilla extract

TOPPING

10 to 12 fresh figs, sliced in half

½ cup salted pistachios, shelled and coarsely chopped

3 tablespoons turbinado or granulated sugar

PEACH AND ALMOND
CREAM CHEESE POUND CAKE

MAKES ONE 9 × 5-INCH LOAF

A classic pound cake with a fruity bend, I love a thick slice of this cake with a cup of tea. With both cream cheese and butter, this cake is both dense and moist. While it takes some serious quality time in the oven, because it's so rich, it is forgiving if it gets a few minutes of overbaking.

1. Place a rack in the center of the oven and preheat the oven to 325°F. Grease a 9 × 5-inch baking pan and dust with flour.

2. In a medium bowl, whisk together the flour, baking powder, baking soda, and salt.

3. In the bowl of an electric mixer fitted with the paddle attachment, beat together the butter and cream cheese. Scrape down the sides of the bowl. Add the sugars and beat on medium speed until smooth and creamy, about 3 minutes. Scrape down the sides of the bowl. Turn the mixer on medium speed and add the eggs, one at a time, beating for 1 minute after each addition. Beat in the vanilla and almond extracts. Add the flour mixture and beat on low speed until incorporated. Spoon the batter into the prepared pan. Top with the sliced peaches and sliced almonds.

4. Bake, rotating once or twice during baking, for 50 to 60 minutes, until a toothpick inserted in the center comes out clean or with just a few crumbs. If the loaf is browning too quickly, place a foil tent over the cake after about 45 minutes of baking.

5. The cake will last for up to 4 days, well wrapped, at room temperature.

¾ cup (1½ sticks) unsalted butter, at room temperature, plus more for the pan

2 cups all-purpose flour, plus more for the pan

1½ teaspoons baking powder

½ teaspoon baking soda

½ teaspoon salt

1 (8-ounce) package cream cheese, at room temperature

1 cup granulated sugar

½ cup packed light brown sugar

4 large eggs

2 teaspoons pure vanilla extract

½ teaspoon pure almond extract

1 ripe peach, pitted and thinly sliced

½ cup sliced almonds

BLACKBERRY COBBLER MUFFINS
WITH PISTACHIOS

MAKES 12 MUFFINS

Muffins are special. Muffins are small, individual-size cake-for-breakfast situations that deserve a good amount of attention and creativity. Cobbler isn't really a breakfast item—until you make it into a muffin—two desserts in one sweet brunch dish. Fresh blueberries and raspberries are equally delicious, if you'd care to swap out the blackberries.

1. **FOR THE MUFFINS:** Place a rack in the upper third of the oven and preheat to 375°F. Line a twelve-cup muffin tin with liners.

2. In a separate medium bowl, whisk together the flour, sugar, baking powder, cinnamon, nutmeg, and salt.

3. In a medium bowl, whisk together the milk, egg and egg yolk, and vanilla. Add the brown butter and whisk well. Add the mixture all at once to the flour mixture and stir gently to combine. Gently fold in the blackberries. Divide the batter among the muffin cups and spread evenly.

4. **FOR THE TOPPING:** In a medium bowl, combine the butter, flour, sugar, cinnamon, and salt and rub together with your fingertips until crumbly. Toss in the pistachios. Sprinkle evenly over the batter in the tin.

5. Bake for 18 to 20 minutes, until golden; a toothpick inserted into the center of a muffin should come out clean. Transfer to a wire rack for 15 minutes, and then remove the muffins from the pan. The muffins will keep for up to 3 days, well wrapped at room temperature.

MUFFINS

1½ cups all-purpose flour

¾ cup sugar

1½ teaspoons baking powder

½ teaspoon ground cinnamon

¼ teaspoon freshly grated nutmeg

¾ teaspoon salt

⅓ cup whole milk

1 large egg plus 1 large egg yolk

1 teaspoon pure vanilla extract

½ cup Browned Butter (page 97)

1½ cups fresh blackberries, cut in half if large

TOPPING

3 tablespoons cold unsalted butter, cut into ½-inch cubes

½ cup all-purpose flour

3½ tablespoons sugar

½ teaspoon ground cinnamon

¼ teaspoon salt

⅓ cup coarsely chopped roasted, salted pistachios

DAD'S BUTTERMILK BISCUITS

MAKES 12 TO 14 BISCUITS

The business of cookbooks involves giving away treasured family secrets. Really, though, there should be no secrets in the kitchen. These are my dad's buttermilk biscuits. This recipe was a family secret until my dad realized that everyone just wanted him to make them. They didn't want the recipe so much as they wanted the biscuits to just appear on the table, warm with lots of butter. These biscuits are delicious served warm with Vanilla Bean Butter (page 146). Now the family secret is in your hands.

I large egg

¾ cup cold buttermilk

3 cups all-purpose flour, plus more for rolling

2 tablespoons sugar

2½ teaspoons baking powder

½ teaspoon baking soda

¾ teaspoon salt

¾ cup cold salted high-quality butter (I like Plugrá), cut into small cubes, plus 2 tablespoons melted butter for brushing

1. Place a rack in the upper third of the oven and preheat to 400°F. Line a rimmed baking sheet with parchment paper.

2. In a small bowl or liquid measuring cup, combine the egg and buttermilk and beat with a fork.

3. In a medium bowl, sift together the flour, sugar, baking powder, baking soda, and salt.

4. Using your fingers, quickly work the butter into the mixture until some bits of butter are the size of oat flakes and some are the size of small peas. Create a well in the center of the flour mixture and add the egg mixture all at once. Stir into a shaggy dough that's moist but not overly wet.

5. Turn the dough out onto a lightly floured work surface and, using a floured rolling pin, gently roll the dough into a 1-inch-thick oval. Fold the short end of the dough over until the edge of the dough meets the center of the dough. Fold the other short end of the dough toward the center and over the first fold. Gently roll the dough into a 1-inch-thick oval and repeat the folding process again twice more. Again roll the dough out to a 1-inch-thick oval.

6. Use a 2-inch round biscuit cutter (or the top of a small glass) to cut out the biscuits. Reroll the dough scraps and cut out a few more biscuits. Place 1 inch apart on the prepared baking sheet and brush lightly with the melted butter.

7. Bake for 15 to 18 minutes, until golden brown on top. Serve warm, with lots of butter. The biscuits are best the day they're made, though they can also be frozen and lightly reheated in the oven.

CHOCOLATE HAZELNUT
COFFEE CAKE

MAKES ONE 9-INCH CAKE

When I close my eyes and picture my perfect brunch table (something I usually find myself doing most Saturday nights around 7:45), it always includes cake. This recipe takes coffee cake to new heights.

1. **FOR THE TOPPING:** In a medium bowl, combine the flour, brown sugar, cinnamon, and salt. Add the butter and, using your fingers, work the butter into the mixture, creating a crumble with some butter bits about the size of oat flakes still visible. Toss in the chocolate pieces and chopped hazelnuts.

2. **FOR THE CAKE:** Place a rack in the center of the oven and preheat to 350°F. Grease and flour a 9 × 13-inch pan (metal is best).

3. In a medium bowl, whisk together the flour, cocoa powder, baking powder, baking soda, espresso powder if using, cinnamon, and salt.

4. In the bowl of a stand mixer fitted with a paddle attachment, beat the butter and sugar for 3 to 5 minutes, until slightly pale and fluffy. Add the vanilla and beat for 30 seconds. Add the eggs one at a time, and beat for 1 minute between each addition. Add half of the flour mixture and beat on low speed until just incorporated. Scrape down the sides of the bowl and add all of the sour cream. Mix on low until just incorporated. Add the remaining flour mixture and beat on low speed until incorporated. Increase the speed to medium and beat for 1 more minute. Scrape the batter into the prepared pan. Scatter the topping over the batter and use a butter knife to swirl just slightly.

5. Bake 40 to 45 minutes, until a skewer inserted in the center comes out with just a few moist crumbs. Let cool slightly. Drizzle with melted chocolate, if you'd like, before serving. The cake will keep for up to 5 days, well wrapped, at room temperature.

TOPPING

½ cup all-purpose flour

½ cup lightly packed light brown sugar

1 teaspoon ground cinnamon

¼ teaspoon salt

6 tablespoons cold unsalted butter, cut into cubes

½ cup coarsely chopped dark chocolate or dark chocolate chips

¾ cup coarsely chopped hazelnuts

CAKE

½ cup (1 stick) unsalted butter, softened, plus more for the pan

2 cups all-purpose flour, plus more for the pan

⅔ cup unsweetened cocoa powder

1 teaspoon baking powder

1 teaspoon baking soda

1 teaspoon instant espresso powder (optional)

½ teaspoon ground cinnamon

½ teaspoon salt

1 cup lightly packed brown sugar

1 tablespoon pure vanilla extract

3 large eggs

1 cup sour cream

⅓ cup melted dark chocolate, for topping (optional)

FRESH CRANBERRY AND ORANGE
SCONES

MAKES 8 SCONES

I love the play of tart cranberries with bright, clean orange in these sweet scones. Cranberries are winter jewels, beautiful in color and bold in flavor. These scones are best made during the colder months, when fresh cranberries are readily available (unless you're the genius who stashed a fresh bag away in the freezer). Dried cranberries will do in a pinch, but they're much sweeter than fresh ones, so the scones won't have that tart bite.

1. **FOR THE SCONES:** In a medium bowl, combine the flour, sugar, baking powder, baking soda, and salt. Add the butter and, using your hands, quickly break it up into the flour mixture until some pieces of butter are the size of small peas and others are the size of oat flakes.

2. In a small bowl, whisk together the egg, buttermilk, and orange zest. Add the egg mixture to the flour mixture and, using a wooden spoon, stir until the dough just comes together. Stir in the cranberries. Knead the dough about 20 turns, until it comes together in a cohesive disk. Turn the dough out onto a lightly floured work surface and press it into a disk. Wrap in plastic wrap and refrigerate for 1 hour or overnight.

SCONES

2¼ cups all-purpose flour, plus more for rolling

3 tablespoons granulated sugar

1 teaspoon baking powder

½ teaspoon baking soda

½ teaspoon salt

½ cup (1 stick) cold unsalted butter, cut into small cubes

1 large egg

½ cup cold buttermilk

2 teaspoons grated orange zest

1 heaping cup fresh cranberries, some cut in half and some left whole

1 large egg, beaten

GLAZE

2 to 3 tablespoons fresh orange juice

½ teaspoon pure vanilla extract

1 cup confectioners' sugar

½ teaspoon grated orange zest

Pinch of salt

(recipe continues)

3. Place a rack in the upper third of the oven and preheat the oven to 375°F. Line a rimmed baking sheet with parchment paper.

4. Unwrap the dough, place it on the prepared baking sheet, and press it into a 1½-inch-thick circle. Using a large knife, cut the dough into eight wedges and separate the wedges by about ½ inch. Brush lightly with the beaten egg.

5. Bake for 15 to 18 minutes, until the scones are golden brown and some of the cranberries have burst. The scones will expand as they bake and stick together. That's all right. Let cool to just warm.

6. FOR THE GLAZE: In a small bowl, whisk together 2 tablespoons of orange juice with the vanilla, confectioners' sugar, orange zest, and salt. Add the remaining 1 tablespoon orange juice if you'd like a looser glaze.

7. Drizzle the scones with the glaze and serve slightly warm. The scones are best served the day they're made.

STRAWBERRY SHORTCAKE
DOUGHNUTS

MAKES 12 DOUGHNUTS

When I was a kid, strawberry shortcake signified a very special Friday night. Someone must have come home with a good report card to warrant such a treat. Here, I've taken our Friday-night childhood splurge dessert to the breakfast table. Forget yellow cake—this is all about tender, fluffy doughnuts stuffed with house-whipped cream and sweet berries. This is as good as it gets!

1. **FOR THE DOUGHNUTS:** In the bowl of a stand mixer fitted with a dough hook, stir together the yeast and warm water until the yeast has dissolved. Let it rest for 5 minutes, until foamy.

2. To the yeast, add the warm milk, butter, egg yolks, flour, sugar, and salt. Turn the mixer on low speed and mix for about 5 minutes, until a soft dough forms. Increase the speed to medium-high and beat for 3 more minutes, until the dough begins to pull away from the sides of the bowl. Stop the mixer, remove the dough hook, and gather the dough in the center of the bowl. Sprinkle the top of the dough with flour to keep a crust from forming. Cover the bowl with plastic wrap and let the dough rise in a draft-free place at warm room temperature until doubled in bulk, 1½ to 2 hours. (Alternatively, let it rise in the refrigerator for 8 to 12 hours.)

3. Turn the dough out onto a lightly floured work surface and, using a lightly floured rolling pin, roll it out into a 12-inch round that's ½ inch thick. Using a 3-inch round cutter, cut out as many circles as you can and put them onto a lightly floured baking sheet. Cover the doughnuts with a kitchen towel and let rise in a draft-free place at warm room temperature until slightly puffed, about 30 minutes (45 minutes, if the dough was cold when cutting out the doughnuts). Do not reroll the scraps; they'll be tough.

DOUGHNUTS
2¼ teaspoons (1 package) active dry yeast

2 tablespoons warm water

1 cup whole milk, warm

¼ cup unsalted butter, at room temperature

3 large egg yolks

3¼ cups all-purpose flour, plus more for dusting

2 tablespoons granulated sugar

1½ teaspoons salt

2 quarts canola oil, for frying

STRAWBERRIES
1 pound fresh strawberries, hulled and sliced

3 tablespoons granulated sugar

WHIPPED CREAM
2 cups heavy cream

1 teaspoon pure vanilla extract

2 tablespoons confectioners' sugar

GLAZE
2 cups confectioners' sugar

2 to 3 tablespoons whole milk

1 teaspoon pure vanilla extract

Pinch of salt

(recipe continues)

4. **FOR THE STRAWBERRIES:** In a small bowl, combine the strawberries and sugar. Let sit for 20 minutes at room temperature.

5. **FOR THE WHIPPED CREAM:** In the bowl of a stand mixer fitted with a whisk attachment, beat together the cream, vanilla, and confectioners' sugar.

6. **FOR THE GLAZE:** In a small bowl, whisk together the confectioners' sugar, 2 tablespoons of milk, vanilla, and salt. Add more milk, if needed, to make a thick but pourable glaze.

7. In a medium saucepan fitted with a deep-fry thermometer and set over medium heat, heat about 2½ inches of oil to 350°F. Working in batches of two, fry for about 2 minutes total, turning occasionally, until puffed and golden brown. Transfer to a paper towel–lined plate to drain. Return the oil to 350°F between each batch.

8. I like to assemble these doughnuts right before serving. To assemble, slice horizontally through each doughnut, leaving the end of each doughnut uncut so the doughnut stays together. Dollop whipped cream and strawberries inside each doughnut and sandwich together. Top with glaze and enjoy immediately. The doughnuts are best the day they're made.

SUPER-SEEDED
PUMPKIN CAKE BREAD

MAKES 1 LOAF

Pumpkin is our fall baking multitasker, and it adds its flavor, moisture, and beautiful golden color to this loaf cake. I thought we'd go big with loads of spice in the bread, and a top crust filled with nuts and seeds. Basically, empty the spice cupboard and the seed drawer into a mixing bowl. It's going to be good. Served with softened butter and a drizzle of honey, it's truly a treat. (See photograph, page 196.)

1. Place a rack in the center of the oven and preheat the oven to 350°F. Grease and flour a 9 × 5-inch loaf pan.

2. In a medium bowl, whisk together the flour, baking soda, baking powder, pumpkin pie spice, cinnamon, nutmeg, cardamom, salt, and pepper.

3. In the bowl of a stand mixer fitted with a paddle attachment, beat the butter and brown sugar for 3 to 5 minutes, until slightly pale and fluffy. Beat in the eggs one at a time, and beat for 1 minute between each addition. Add the pumpkin purée and beat until combined. Add the buttermilk and vanilla and beat well. Add in the flour mixture and beat on low speed until almost completely combined.

4. Remove the bowl from the mixer and finish incorporating the flour using a spatula or wooden spoon. Spoon the batter into the prepared pan. Sprinkle with the walnuts, pecans, pumpkin seeds, sunflower seeds, and millet. Using a butter knife, swirl the nuts and seeds into the batter slightly.

5. Bake for 45 to 55 minutes, until a toothpick inserted in the bread comes out clean. Let cool for 15 minutes before transferring to a wire rack to cool. Serve warm.

½ cup (1 stick) unsalted butter, at room temperature, plus more for the pan

2 cups all-purpose flour, plus more for the pan

1 teaspoon baking soda

½ teaspoon baking powder

1½ teaspoons pumpkin pie spice

½ teaspoon ground cinnamon

¼ teaspoon freshly grated nutmeg

¼ teaspoon ground cardamom

½ teaspoon salt

Generous pinch of freshly ground black pepper

1 cup packed light brown sugar

2 large eggs

1 cup canned pumpkin purée

⅓ cup buttermilk

2 teaspoons pure vanilla extract

¼ cup coarsely chopped walnuts

¼ cup coarsely chopped pecans

¼ cup roasted pumpkin seeds

2 tablespoons salted sunflower seeds

1 tablespoon millet

VERY STICKY PECAN ROLLS

MAKES 12 LARGE ROLLS

There's no easy way around it. If you want real-deal sticky buns, you have to earn them. By that, I mean you'll need to take out your stand mixer, a lot of mixing bowls, and all of the butter in your refrigerator. There are three major steps to making these rolls, but they still manage to be fairly approachable. Worth it?! One hundred percent.

1. **FOR THE DOUGH:** In the bowl of a stand mixer, combine the yeast, granulated sugar, and water. Stir to combine and let sit for about 10 minutes, until foamy.

2. To the yeast mixture, add the brown sugar, milk, vanilla, egg, and egg yolk. Whisk together until well combined.

3. Fit the bowl onto the mixer and attach the dough hook. Add the flour and salt and mix on medium speed for about 4 minutes, until the dough just begins to come together. Increase the speed to medium-high and knead the dough until it begins to pull away from the sides of the bowl, 4 minutes. Add the butter in chunks and continue to knead until the dough is slightly sticky and wet, about 6 minutes.

4. Transfer to a well-floured work surface, and knead by hand. Don't worry, the dough still might be a little sticky. It's okay. Put the dough in a large greased bowl, cover the bowl with plastic wrap, and let it rise in a warm place for 1½ to 2 hours, until doubled in size.

5. **FOR THE FILLING:** In a large bowl, combine the brown sugar, cinnamon, nutmeg, cloves, and salt.

DOUGH

2¼ teaspoons (1 package) active dry yeast

½ teaspoon granulated sugar

¼ cup warm water (115°F)

⅓ cup lightly packed light brown sugar

½ cup whole milk, at room temperature

1 teaspoon pure vanilla extract

1 large egg, lightly beaten, plus 1 large egg yolk

3 cups all-purpose flour, plus more for kneading

½ teaspoon salt

4 tablespoons unsalted butter (½ stick), at room temperature, cut into cubes, plus more for the bowl

FILLING

½ cup packed light brown sugar

1 tablespoon ground cinnamon

1 teaspoon freshly grated nutmeg

⅛ teaspoon ground cloves

½ teaspoon salt

8 tablespoons (1 stick) unsalted butter, melted and cooled slightly

(recipe continues)

6. **FOR THE TOPPING:** In a medium saucepan set over medium heat, combine the cream, honey, butter, sugar, and salt. Cook, whisking, for about 4 minutes, until the mixture is bubbling slightly. Pour half of the syrup into a greased 9 × 13-inch pan and tilt the pan to coat the bottom. Sprinkle 1 cup of pecans into the pan. Stir the remaining pecans into the remaining syrup and set aside.

7. To assemble, unwrap the dough and dump it onto a well-floured work surface. Gently knead the dough until it is no longer sticky, adding a bit more flour as needed, 1 to 2 minutes. Cover with a kitchen towel and let rest for 5 minutes.

8. Using a floured rolling pin, roll the dough into a 12 × 15-inch rectangle. Brush the top of the dough with the melted butter.

9. Sprinkle the filling evenly over the dough, leaving a 1-inch border at one of the short edges. Lightly press the filling into the dough. Using your hands, lift up the bottom edge of the dough and roll it into a tight log. Transfer the dough, seam side down, to a cutting board. Using a sharp, thin knife, trim off the uneven edges and discard them. Cut the log into twelve equal slices. Nestle the slices, cut side up, into the nuts and syrup in the pan. Cover with plastic wrap and set aside in a warm place to let rise for 30 minutes. You may also refrigerate the rolls overnight.

10. Preheat the oven to 375°F. Uncover the rolls. (If you refrigerated them, let them sit at room temperature for 15 minutes before baking.) Bake for about 30 minutes, until golden brown; a toothpick inserted in the center should come out clean. Let cool for 10 minutes. Carefully invert the rolls (while still warm) onto a large platter. Top with the remaining pecan topping and serve warm.

TOPPING

¾ cup heavy cream

½ cup honey

4 tablespoons (½ stick) unsalted butter, plus more for the pan

½ cup packed light brown sugar

½ teaspoon salt

2 cups coarsely chopped pecans

LEMON POPPY SEED PALMIERS

MAKES 22 TO 24 PALMIERS

The key to a good palmier is very crispy puff pastry and a caramelized sugar bottom. The lemon and poppy seeds add a brunchy twist, making these cookies lovely served with tea before noon. Poppy seeds are deceivingly delicate; their oils can go rancid rather quickly. I keep my poppy seeds in an airtight resealable plastic bag in the freezer, rather than the spice cabinet, for freshness.

1 scant cup sugar

1 tablespoon grated lemon zest

1 tablespoon poppy seeds

Pinch of salt

1 sheet rectangular all-butter puff pastry, thawed but still cool (I like Dufour)

1. In a medium bowl, combine the sugar and the lemon zest, using the back of a spoon to rub the zest into the sugar. Sprinkle about half of the lemon sugar onto a clean work surface. Stir the poppy seeds and salt into the remaining lemon sugar in the bowl.

2. On the work surface, unfold the puff pastry on top of the lemon sugar and then flip the pastry to lightly coat both sides. Using a rolling pin, roll out the puff pastry, extending the rectangle by about ½ inch on all sides. (If the pastry tears a bit, just press back together with your fingers.) Sprinkle evenly with the poppy seed mixture. Roll the left vertical side of the pastry toward the center seam, then roll the right vertical side toward the center. Gently press the sides together. Wrap in plastic wrap and refrigerate for 1 hour, until cold and firm.

3. Place racks in the center and upper third of the oven and preheat to 400°F. Line two rimmed baking sheets with parchment paper.

4. Unwrap the dough and cut it into ½-inch slices. Place the cookies about 1 inch apart on the prepared baking sheets.

5. Bake for 11 to 14 minutes, until golden brown around the edges. You may want to rotate the baking sheets halfway through baking. And keep an eye on the cookies, as the sugar can burn quickly. Let cool for 15 minutes before removing from the pan. The cookies will keep for 1 week in an airtight container at room temperature.

JAM PINWHEELS

MAKES 12 COOKIES

All-butter puff pastry is like a genie in a bottle ready to grant your every kitchen wish. It's just so versatile, and very easy to work with. Pairing buttery puff pastry with very good jam is a slam-dunk. Shape it and bake it and call it a cookie, perfect for eating with milky tea in the early afternoon.

All-purpose flour, for the work surface

I package all-butter puff pastry, thawed but still cold (I like Dufour)

I cup good-quality jam

Confectioners' sugar, for dusting

1. Place a rack in the center and upper third of the oven and preheat to 375°F. Line two rimmed baking sheets with parchment paper.

2. Unfold the puff pastry on a lightly floured work surface and cut it into 4-inch squares. Spoon 1 tablespoon of the jam into the center of each square. Using a sharp knife, cut diagonally from each corner of the squares into the center, coming within about ½ inch of the jam. Fold the other corners up to the center of the jam and pinch the points together.

3. Bake until puffed and golden brown, 18 to 20 minutes. Let cool on the baking sheet for 5 minutes before transferring to a wire rack to cool completely.

4. Once cooled, dust with confectioners' sugar before serving. The cookies will last for 3 days in an airtight container at room temperature.

BROWN-BUTTER DOUGHNUTS
WITH BROWN-BUTTER GLAZE

MAKES 16 TO 18 DOUGHNUTS

"More is more is exactly enough" is my motto when it comes to brown butter. These soft, cakey baked doughnuts are loaded with butter that's browned and nutty and fragrant. With a little bit of nutmeg here and there, these doughnuts are all dressed up for brunch.

1. FOR THE DOUGHNUTS: In the bowl of a stand mixer fitted with the dough hook attachment, stir together the yeast and warm water until the yeast dissolves. Let stand for about 5 minutes, until foamy.

2. Add the brown butter, milk, egg yolks, flour, sugar, nutmeg, and salt. On low speed, beat until a soft dough forms. Increase the speed to medium-high and beat for 3 minutes. Scrape down the sides of the bowl. Lightly sprinkle the dough with flour to keep a crust from forming.

3. Cover with a kitchen towel and let rise in a draft-free place at warm room temperature until doubled in size, 1½ to 2 hours. (Alternatively, let it rise in the refrigerator for 8 to 12 hours.)

4. Turn the dough out onto a lightly floured work surface and, using a lightly floured rolling pin, roll it out into a 12-inch circle that is ½ inch thick. Using a 3-inch round cutter, cut out as many rounds as possible and transfer them to a large, lightly floured, rimmed baking sheet. Cover with a kitchen towel and let rise for about 30 minutes (45 minutes if the dough was cold when cutting out the doughnuts) in a draft-free place at warm room temperature, until slightly puffed. Do not reroll the scraps.

DOUGHNUTS

2¼ teaspoons (1 package) active dry yeast

2 tablespoons warm water

¼ cup plus 1 tablespoon Browned Butter (page 97)

1 cup whole milk, warm

3 large egg yolks

3¼ cups all-purpose flour, plus more for dusting

2 tablespoons granulated sugar

½ teaspoon freshly grated nutmeg

1½ teaspoons salt

2 quarts canola oil, for frying

GLAZE

2 cups confectioners' sugar

¼ teaspoon salt

Pinch of freshly grated nutmeg

3 tablespoons Browned Butter (page 97)

1 teaspoon pure vanilla extract

3 to 4 tablespoons whole milk

5. In a deep 4-quart heavy pot fitted with a deep-fry thermometer and set over medium heat, heat 2½ inches of oil to 350°F. Working in batches of two, fry the doughnuts for about 2 minutes total, turning them occasionally, until puffed and golden brown. Transfer to a paper towel–lined plate. Return the oil to 350°F between batches.

6. FOR THE GLAZE: In a medium bowl, whisk together the confectioners' sugar, salt, and nutmeg. Whisk in the brown butter, the vanilla, and the 3 tablespoons of milk. The glaze should be smooth, thin, and pourable. If it's too thick, whisk in the remaining 1 tablespoon milk.

7. Place a wire cooling rack inside a rimmed baking sheet. Dip the doughnuts into the glaze. Transfer to the prepared wire rack and let the glaze set for at least 20 minutes. The doughnuts are best served the day they're made, but they'll keep for 2 days, well wrapped, at room temperature.

BREAKFAST SAUSAGE
PRETZEL ROLLS

MAKES 18 ROLLS

These bites are a play on pigs in a blanket, calling for the more adult (hmm) combinations of breakfast sausage and homemade pretzel dough. Dip in warm maple syrup to add a sweetness to the salty bites, although ketchup is also a great idea.

1½ cups warm water (110°F to 115°F)

1 tablespoon sugar

2¼ teaspoons (1 package) active dry yeast

2 tablespoons unsalted butter, melted and cooled

4½ cups all-purpose flour, plus more for dusting

2 teaspoons salt

Vegetable oil, for brushing

1 cup baking soda

18 fully cooked breakfast sausage links

1 large egg

Flaky salt

Freshly cracked black pepper

1. In the bowl of a stand mixer fitted with a dough hook, combine the warm water and sugar. Sprinkle the yeast on top and let sit for 5 minutes, until foamy. Add the butter, flour, and salt. Mix on low speed until combined. Increase the speed to medium and knead for 4 minutes, until it's smooth and pulls away from the bowl. Sprinkle with flour, cover with plastic wrap, and store in a warm place to rise until doubled in size, 1½ to 2 hours.

2. Place racks in the center and upper third of the oven and preheat to 425°F. Line two rimmed baking sheets with parchment paper and lightly brush the paper with oil (the pretzels like to stick).

3. In a large saucepan set over medium heat bring 10 cups of water to a simmer. Add the baking soda and bring to a boil.

4. Turn the dough out onto a lightly oiled work surface. Divide into 18 pieces. Starting with the fingers of both hands in the center of one piece, roll it, moving your hands away from you, until you have a 10-inch-long rope. Wrap the dough around a sausage link, sealing the ends. Repeat for the remaining pretzels.

5. Working in batches of four at a time, boil a few pretzels for 30 seconds. Using a slotted spatula, transfer to the prepared baking sheets. Beat the egg with a splash of water and brush the egg wash on the pretzels. Sprinkle with flaky salt and pepper.

6. Bake for 12 to 14 minutes, until deep golden brown. Transfer to a wire rack to cool for a few minutes before serving warm.

BUTTERMILK BISCUITS
WITH BACON AND TOMATO GRAVY

MAKES 12 BISCUITS

The concept for this recipe was gifted to me by a bartender in a Baltimore pizzeria. Her name and the name of the restaurant elude me, but I do remember exactly the way she gestured as she described just how her grandmother made tomato gravy and poured it over warm split biscuits topped with bacon. The trick, she noted and emphasized, is not to get fancy with the gravy. Don't go thinking it needs fresh oregano, because it doesn't. Simplicity is key. Simplicity and bacon fat and cooking advice from grandmothers.

1. **FOR THE BACON:** Place a rack in the upper third of the oven and preheat to 375°F.

2. Line a rimmed baking sheet with foil and arrange the bacon on the sheet in one layer. Sprinkle with the sugar. Bake for 15 to 18 minutes, until crisp. Transfer the bacon to a plate to cool. Reserve 2 tablespoons of bacon grease.

3. Increase the oven temperature to 400°F.

4. **FOR THE BISCUITS:** In a medium bowl, whisk together the self-rising flour, sugar, salt, and pepper. Add the chilled butter and, using your fingers or a pastry cutter, work the butter into the flour mixture until the butter is the size of small peas. Add the buttermilk and, using a fork, gently bring the dough together. Transfer to a lightly floured work surface and gently knead the dough into a rectangle. Press or roll the dough until it is about ¾ inch thick. Using a 2-inch round biscuit cutter (or the top of a small glass), cut out as many biscuits as you can. Transfer them to a parchment-lined rimmed baking sheet about 2 inches apart. Don't reroll the scraps. Brush the biscuits with the beaten egg.

BACON
12 thick cut slices bacon

2 tablespoons lightly packed brown sugar

BISCUITS
2 cups self-rising flour

1 tablespoon lightly packed brown sugar

½ teaspoon salt

¼ teaspoon freshly cracked black pepper

4 tablespoons unsalted butter, cold, cut into cubes

¾ cup cold buttermilk

1 large egg, beaten

All-purpose flour, for kneading

TOMATO GRAVY
½ cup chopped yellow onion

1 tablespoon all-purpose flour

1 (14.5-ounce) can diced tomatoes

Salt

Freshly cracked black pepper

¼ cup whole milk

Salted softened butter, for serving

(recipe continues)

5. Bake for 18 to 20 minutes, until golden brown. Let cool.

6. **FOR THE TOMATO GRAVY:** In a medium saucepan set over medium heat, add the reserved bacon fat. Add the onions and cook, stirring, for about 8 minutes, until translucent and lightly browned. Add the flour and cook for 1 minute, stirring constantly. Add the tomatoes, salt, and pepper and simmer for about 8 minutes, until warmed through and thickened. Stir in the milk and simmer for 1 more minute.

7. Cut the warm biscuits in half. Spread each with softened butter. Cut the bacon slices in half and top each biscuit half with a piece of bacon. Spoon the tomato gravy over each bacon slice. Serve immediately.

LAVENDER EGG BREAD

MAKES 1 LOAF

Fragrant, herbal lavender notes are lovely in this egg bread and make it both bold and feminine. It makes wonderful toast, especially when accented with a light spread of Vanilla Bean Butter (page 146), but its true calling is in eggy, griddle-fried French toast.

6 tablespoons butter, plus more for the bowl

½ cup whole milk

¼ cup honey

1½ tablespoons dried lavender

1 tablespoon (1 package plus ½ teaspoon) active dry yeast

3 large eggs, at room temperature

3½ to 4 cups all-purpose flour

1½ teaspoons salt

Canola oil, for the work surface

Nonstick cooking oil spray

1. In a small saucepan set over low heat, melt the butter. Add the milk, honey, and lavender and stir until the honey is dissolved. Remove the pan from the heat and let cool to just above room temperature, about 110°F.

2. Transfer the milk mixture to the bowl of a stand mixer fitted with the dough hook attachment and sprinkle the yeast over the mixture. Add 2 of the eggs, 3½ cups flour, salt, and yeast. Beat on medium speed until it forms a soft, smooth dough, 8 to 10 minutes. Add the remaining flour if you find the dough is too sticky.

3. Lightly butter a large bowl. Place the dough in the bowl, cover with plastic wrap, and let it rise for 1½ to 2 hours in a warm place, until doubled in size.

4. Transfer the dough to a lightly oiled work surface and divide it into three equal pieces. Gently roll and stretch each piece into a 15-inch rope. Cover with a kitchen towel and let rest for 10 minutes.

5. Continue rolling each rope until it is about 18 inches long. Lay the three ropes parallel to one another and pinch them together at the top. Lightly and gently braid the ropes, then pinch the ends of the large rope together and tuck under.

(recipe continues)

6. Line a rimmed baking sheet with parchment paper and lightly spritz with nonstick cooking spray. Carefully transfer the braid to the prepared pan. Cover it with plastic wrap that's been lightly spritzed with nonstick cooking spray and let rise again for 1 hour, until the loaf has increased by about half.

7. Place a rack in the center of the oven and preheat to 375°F.

8. Beat the remaining egg, and lightly brush the loaf with the egg wash. Place the baking sheet that the loaf is on inside another baking sheet to insulate the bottom of the loaf so that it won't brown too quickly.

9. Bake for 20 minutes, and then lightly cover the loaf with foil. Bake for 20 to 25 minutes, until the loaf is a deep golden brown and sounds a bit hollow when it tapped. Let cool completely before slicing and serving.

OLIVE OIL FLATBREAD

MAKES 1 LARGE FLATBREAD

I love the rusticity and flexibility of flatbread. Shaped with our hands, bathed in olive oil, baked until beautifully browned, and topped with any sweet or savory combination our heart desires. I like this bread topped with sweet red grapes, or with roasted tomatoes, a fragrant herb, and loads of pepper and sea salt.

1. **FOR THE FLATBREAD:** In a large bowl, sprinkle the yeast over ½ cup of the warm water. Add a pinch of sugar and let sit for 5 minutes, until foamy.

2. Add the remaining ½ cup water, the remaining 3 tablespoons sugar, 2 cups of flour, the olive oil, and salt. Using a wooden spoon, stir well. Add the remaining 1 cup flour, ¼ cup at a time, until the dough comes together. Transfer the dough to a lightly floured work surface and knead for 5 minutes. The dough should be sticky, but if it's too sticky, add up to ⅓ cup more flour while kneading.

3. Coat a clean large bowl with a splash of olive oil. Place the dough in the bowl and flip it over until it's entirely coated in oil. Cover and let rise for 1½ to 2 hours in a warm place, until doubled in size.

4. Punch the dough down and transfer to a very lightly floured work surface. Knead for 1 minute, before pulling and stretching the dough into a 16 × 9-inch rectangle. (I use a rolling pin.) Generously grease a rimmed baking sheet with olive oil, transfer the dough to the baking sheet, and let rise for 30 minutes.

FLATBREAD

2¼ teaspoons (1 package) active dry yeast

1 cup warm water (110°F to 115°F)

3 tablespoons plus a pinch of sugar

3 cups all-purpose flour, plus more for kneading

3 tablespoons olive oil, plus more for the bowl, baking sheet, and drizzling

1¼ teaspoons salt

TOPPING COMBINATIONS
(pick one or the other)

Red grapes, fresh rosemary, freshly cracked black pepper, sea salt

Roasted tomatoes, fresh basil, Parmesan cheese, freshly cracked black pepper, sea salt

5. Place a rack in the center of the oven and preheat to 375°F.

6. Using your fingers, make random indentations in the dough.
    Drizzle with olive oil and add any toppings.

7. Bake, rotating the baking sheet after 15 minutes, until golden,
    crisp, and baked through, 30 to 35 minutes. Let cool for 10
    minutes. Remove the flatbread from the baking sheet, slice into
    squares with a pizza cutter, and serve. The flatbread is best served
    within 2 days of baking.

SPINACH AND ARTICHOKE
STRATA

SERVES 6 TO 8

Strata is essentially a savory bread pudding. Hearty with vegetables, dense with bread, yet with a light and fluffy texture thanks to whipped eggs and cream, it's a meal in its own right. This is a great dish to serve to a crowd with a batch of micheladas (page 13) and Spicy Brown Sugar Sausage Patties (page 135). Bonus! You can assemble this recipe the night before and refrigerate it overnight.

1. Generously butter a 3-quart gratin or casserole dish and set aside.

2. In a medium skillet set over medium heat, heat the clarified butter and the olive oil. Add the onions and cook for about 5 minutes, until softened and translucent. Add the spinach and artichoke and stir well, heating through.

3. Place one-third of the bread cubes in the prepared baking dish. Top with one-third of the spinach-artichoke mixture and one-third of the cheese. Repeat the layering, finishing with cheese.

4. In a large bowl, whisk together the milk, cream, mustard, eggs, nutmeg, salt, and pepper. Pour the mixture over the bread and spinach in the pan. Cover with plastic wrap and refrigerate for at least 1 hour, though overnight is best.

5. Place a rack in the center of the oven and preheat to 350°F.

6. If the strata was refrigerated for 1 hour, bake right from the refrigerator. If it was refrigerated overnight, let it sit at room temperature for 20 minutes.

7. Bake the strata until cooked through and golden brown, 45 to 55 minutes. Let cool for at least 15 minutes before serving. Strata is best served warm or at room temperature.

Softened butter, for the dish

2 tablespoons Clarified Butter (page 57)

2 tablespoons olive oil

I large onion, chopped

I (10-ounce) package frozen spinach, thawed, excess liquid squeezed out, coarsely chopped

I (15-ounce) can artichoke hearts, drained and coarsely chopped

8 cups sourdough bread cubes

2 cups coarsely grated Gruyère cheese

2 cups whole milk

½ cup heavy cream

2 tablespoons whole-grain mustard

8 large eggs

Pinch of freshly grated nutmeg

I teaspoon salt

½ teaspoon freshly cracked black pepper

ACKNOWLEDGMENTS

It is with deep care and ravenous appreciation that I thank each and every one of you who has pulled up a recipe from joythebaker.com and set off to your kitchen. The community of butter enthusiasts, chocolate hoarders, and doughnut creators we've become together is astounding, inspiring, and downright silly. I thank you for sharing in and feeding my passion.

Jon, thank you for envisioning this book with me and holding a camera to all of my harebrained cocktail and pancake ideas without ever batting an eyelash.

Kari Stuart and Ashley Meyer, high-five and fist-pump. We made another beautiful book together! Thank you for caring about words, images, eggs, and grits as much as I do. I feel deeply fortunate to work with such strong, clear, life-loving women such as you two. Thanks also to Aaron Wehner, Doris Cooper, and La Tricia Watford at Clarkson Potter.

Thank you to my family! My fear of soft-boiled eggs was born with you, but so was my love of biscuits. Love wins. Your support and pride make life worth living and brunch worth serving.

My maj Tracy, Whitney, Sister, Lauren, and Cara: Thank you for helping me know when to shut up, buck up, carry on, and settle up. Aside from the side-splitting, life-giving laughter, your friendship and encouragement is a blessing to my life and, hallelujah, I'm thankful for you all!

Amos, thank you for sharing your breakfasts and your food brain with me. Your big heart keeps me.

Thank you, coffee; thank you, spell check; thank you, yoga; thank you, long walks; thank you, pep talks; thank you, Pizza Delicious in New Orleans for the pizza breaks and sanity wine. We're good. We made it.

INDEX

Note: Page references in *italics* indicate photographs.

JOY WILSON is well known for her daily dabbles in butter and sugar as her blogging alter ego, Joy the Baker. Since its launch in 2008, *Joy the Baker* has received many accolades, including being selected as one of the 50 Best Food Blogs by *The Times* (London) and named Best Baking and Desserts Blog by *Saveur*. Joy's content has also been featured on sites such as *Food52, The Kitchn,* and Buzzfeed.

A native California girl, Joy now lives in New Orleans with her big orange cat, Tron. When she's not baking, blogging, or Instagramming, she's searching for the best Sazerac in town or finding her zen in yoga class.